Stigmata

By the same author

ELVIS PEOPLE

Stigmata

A Medieval Mystery in a Modern Age

TED HARRISON

St. Martin's Press
New York

Library of Congress Cataloging-in-Publication Data

Harrison, Ted.
Stigmata / Ted Harrison.
p. cm.
ISBN 0-312-11372-2 (hardcover)
1. Stigmatization. I. Title.
BV5091.S7H37 1994
248.2'9—dc20 94-21367 CIP

First published in Great Britain by Fount Paperbacks.

First U.S. Edition: October 1994
10 9 8 7 6 5 4 3 2 1

Contents

Acknowledgements

I have been interested in the study of stigmata since my meeting in the late seventies with the late Ethel Chapman. Over that period many people have assisted in the process of forming the view of the subject I now subscribe to. These people include Ethel herself, Jane Hunt, George H., Father Jim Bruse and Heather Woods, the stigmatists I have known personally and some of their spiritual or medical advisers. Here I would mention in particular the Rev. David Lockyer, Dr John Spence, the Rev. Norman Hill and the late Bishop Eric Eades. I have also gained considerably from being able to discuss ideas and derive new leads from Dr Peter Moore of the University of Kent at Canterbury. I am grateful too for being able to compare notes with Ian Wilson, and my thanks go to the many librarians who have given of their expertise to enable me to find some obscure works. Finally my special thanks go, for her patience and cheerfulness, to my secretary and assistant, my daughter Caroline.

Ted Harrison, Conyer, Kent.
August 1993

Introduction

In 1937 Eva McIsaac, a devout Roman Catholic from Uptergrove, eighty miles north of Ontario, the granddaughter of a native American, received a small painful mark on the back of her right hand. Within three years the mark had grown and spread, becoming deep and painful. A second mark appeared on her left hand, as did a wound in her side and marks through her feet. Across her back were reddish marks like those made by a lash. They flared up and bled every Friday, becoming particularly active from Maundy Thursday to Good Friday. She had received the stigmata.

On March 17, 1972, Cloretta Robinson, a young Afro-American from West Oakland in California, found herself bleeding from the palm of her left hand. Later, marks appeared on her right hand, feet, and forehead in the days leading up to Easter. She too had had a physical experience of the wounds of Christ's death by execution.

Eva and Cloretta are just two of the small group of people in history who have received these extraordinary marks of crucifixion. They are especially unusual in being two of an even smaller group of people from outside Europe to have received the signs of Christ's suffering on their own person.

When St. Francis of Assisi received replicas of the wounds of Christ on his hands, feet, and right side while on retreat on the slopes of Mount Alvernia in Italy in 1224, the existence of the New World was not even rumored in the Old.

Thus for the first centuries of the history of the stigmata, the phenomenon was unknown outside Europe. It emerged from a religious climate, which was peculiarly Roman Catholic and Mediterranean, in which a devotion to the suffering and Passion of Christ received what many might consider disproportionate emphasis.

The early migrants to America, the Pilgrim Fathers and others, came from a Protestant Reformation tradition in which such an emotional emphasis would have been entirely alien. It was only later, when the new waves of immigrants arrived from Roman Catholic Europe, that the conditions for the emergence of American stigmatics could be established.

Inevitably that which started as a medieval religious curiosity became replicated in the New World as the traditions of the Catholic faith became established. That particular emphasis on the suffering of Christ, at the root of stigmatic experience in Europe, also spread more widely. Thus America saw the first cases of non-Caucasians receiving the wounds.

More recently other examples of Latin religious enthusiasm have manifested themselves in North America. There have been reports of appearances of the Virgin Mary and weeping statues. Such events indicate the development of a Roman Catholic subculture eager to witness the miraculous and to look for the supernatural intervention of God in the world. Perhaps, as is so often the case in Europe when these things happen, they coincide with periods of economic depression and with hard times. When the material world disappoints, the faithful seek signs of the eternal reassurance of God.

Although the American cases of stigmata have to date been few, indications are that conditions are right for new stigmatics to emerge. As some Charismatic and Pentecostal churches turn from their emphasis in worship on Whitsun and the Holy Spirit to Good Friday and the Incarnation, cases of stigmata can be expected outside the Catholic Church, particularly where Afro-Americans meet to worship. For there, members of the congregations have the experiences of poverty and material need, which have been only too familiar to the peasants of Europe in the countries where stigmatics have been most common.

It should not be suggested that an epidemic of stigmata is on its way, but undoubtedly cases will increase in the same way as they are apparently increasing and spreading in Europe today.

This book attempts to explore the phenomenon and explain its social, medical, and theological meaning, in a world where it is normally assumed that science, technology, and consumerism dominate and dictate the shape of the culture.

ONE

Marks of Crucifixion

In the summer of 1985 something extraordinary happened to Jane Hunt, a woman in her late twenties from Codnor in Derbyshire. Wounds appeared in her hands which resembled the marks of Christ's crucifixion. Her hands hurt and bled as if nails had been driven through them.

Just after Christmas in 1991 an assistant priest at a Roman Catholic church in a respectable suburban neighbourhood not far from Washington DC found bleeding wounds on his wrists. His feet too began to hurt and bleed and a little later a wound in his right side opened up.

Early on Easter morning in 1974 Ethel Chapman, who was a patient at the Birkenhead General Hospital on Merseyside, had a vivid dream. She felt herself being drawn onto a cross and told of the pain of nails being driven through her hands and her feet. When she woke in the morning the nurses who came to bath her noticed her hands were bleeding from wounds in the centre of the palms.

And in May 1992, Heather Woods, a forty-three-year-old widow from Lincoln, found small itching blisters in her hands developed into large round tender areas of skin which periodically seeped blood. Similar marks appeared on her feet and a red crescent appeared on her right side. Twice a red mark has appeared on her forehead in the distinct shape of a cross.

For over seven hundred years there have been individual Christians who have exhibited on their bodies the physical marks of Christ's suffering. They have had wounds in their hands as if nails had been hammered through; their feet similarly have scarred and bled; some have marks on the forehead corresponding to those which might have been made by a crown of thorns; others have had a wound in the side as if they have been speared; or stripes across the back as if from scourging. They carry the stigmata, the marks of Christ's passion.

If one leaves aside a single ambiguous reference made by St Paul, it was well into the third century of the second half of the Christian era before the first cases of stigmata appeared. Yet once the phenomenon had occurred it was to occur regularly for the next seven hundred years. Since the first undisputed case, that of St Francis of Assisi in 1224, some three hundred other Christians, it is estimated, have been the recipients of the wounds.

Although the phenomenon first appeared amidst the religious turmoil of the medieval period, the marks persisted into the age of reason and the modern age of scepticism and disbelief. Today there are perhaps around twenty stigmatics living. The majority, as they have been in history, are Roman Catholics, but the present-day stigmatics include one Baptist, one Anglican and one member of a small Celtic Church.

The history of Christianity is full of stories of miracles, wonder and mystery. Many of the stories require deep faith to be believed and so can be dismissed by the cynic with ease. The stigmata have taken many forms and have appeared in a variety of ways, and while a sceptic can deny that the marks have anything to do with God and can maintain that they appear only on hysterical or unbalanced subjects and are possibly self-inflicted, what cannot be denied is that they exist physically and tangibly.

Few people who have ever seen the marks have remained indifferent to them. They provoke wonder, fear, and awe, as well as scepticism and cynicism; they provoke both belief and disbelief.

Sometimes whole communities are thrown into a state of extravagant religious enthusiasm by a stigmatic emerging in their midst. Sometimes personality cults grow up around the stigmatic and there are rumours and claims of miracles and healings. Such was the case with the celebrated twentieth-century Italian stigmatic Padre Pio whose Masses attracted huge crowds and who had long queues every day of people waiting to make their confession to him. What is difficult to determine is whether it is the stigmatics who encourage the group devotions or whether the stigmatics themselves are a product of waves of piety which can sweep towns or districts. In the case of another twentieth-century priest and stigmatic, the American, Father Jim Bruse, it could be claimed that his marks emerged after the start of a Catholic revival both in his parish and in his country generally. He was in a sense an icon of that revival. Viewed in that way it can be suggested that stigmata, up until now treated as an individual gift from or response to God, may also be understood within the context of a group experience of the Divine.

So what is the church reaction to stigmata? Most stigmatists have been Roman Catholic and it is that Church which is most practical in responding to reports of physical mystical phenomena. It invariably reacts cautiously to individual claims while appearing to accept the general idea.

In 1921 Father Benedict Williamson made a study of 'Supernatural Mysticism'. His work was commended by the then Cardinal Archbishop of Westminster, Cardinal Bourne. Father Williamson's writings express the feelings of many devout Roman Catholics who are unquestioning believers in the supernatural origins of many cases of stigmata.

> The love and suffering of these souls 'oned' with Jesus Crucified, so overflows that the very wounds and marks of their Crucified Lord appear in their mortal bodies. Here we seem to find the clue to one of those marvels of God's power that has most strongly impressed the imagination of human kind; certainly no other supernatural manifestation of an external kind has proved so arresting as this; an altogether extraordinary love of the Crucified, joined to an equally extraordinary desire to be like Him, to feel what He felt, and endure in the body what He endured, as far as such is possible for a creature. Love explains all.

Five years later Monsignor Albert Farges, a Roman Catholic theologian from Paris, wrote a treatise on mystical theology in which he contrasted the phenomena which he defined as being of divine origin with those he described as human or diabolical counterfeits. His work was commended to the Church by Pope Benedict XV.

Cautious as ever in such matters, Mgr Farges set out an official church line. The stigmata could be genuine, but in declaring any case to be genuine, considerable care had to be taken. He took the cases of recognized saints who were safely distanced from his day by the passage of time to demonstrate that the stigmata could be a sign of God's favour. The Catholic Church, he said, after many long canonical and medical inquiries, has not feared the danger of 'compromising her divine authority by proclaiming as miraculous the stigmata of St Francis, St Clare of Montefalco, St Catherine of Siena, St Teresa, St Veronica Giuliani, and of many others, by instituting special feasts'. Mgr Farges used the term stigmata very loosely to include any mystical phenomenon which could be taken to be a 'mark' of favour.

He did however make a special point of considering the possibility that the human mind and other medical causes could provide an explanation for stigmata in many other cases and this included an examination of the role of hypnotism.

Mgr Farges also concluded that some false stigmata 'are counterfeits due to the action of the devil, who in all ages, has shown himself to be "the ape of God"; these are always unmasked by their moral malice, as are false ecstasies and false miracles'.

What can be safely said in studying the Roman Catholic Church's response to any current claims of mystical events is that, while approaching every claim with caution and refraining from instant judgements, it is prepared to acknowledge the validity of many claims once a suitable and safe passage of time has elapsed.

Other students of stigmata have approached the phenomenon very differently. Many have not been Roman Catholics and some have even had no religious motivation in making their study. Yet a number of medical doctors in the twentieth century, who have had cause to examine patients with the wounds, have been fascinated by the challenge of finding an explanation.

In 1980 in the specialist publication *Seminars in Haematology*, Dr Oscar Ratnoff of the University Hospitals of Cleveland, Ohio reviewed the historical cases from the modern western viewpoint. He left the question very open, concluding his examination of stigmata and other forms of psychosomatic bruising and lesions with the words 'we have as yet no inkling how emotional pressures can bring about obvious organic results.' At no time did he disbelieve the evidence, but his viewpoint did not allow him to consider the possibilities of a supernatural explanation.

For the individual, however pious and dedicated to their faith, to receive the painful injuries of Christ's suffering and execution on their own bodies is inevitably a shock. The trauma is then compounded by the reaction of others. Some stigmatists have been told to their face that they have been marked by the Devil. In more recent times individuals with the marks have been subjected to close and intimate examination by doctors and psychiatrists. It has been inferred that they have a mental illness and have been labelled as suffering from schizophrenia or hysteria, whatever is the fashionable label at the time. Their faith and spiritual lives have been similarly dissected by parish priests and Vatican envoys. Often those who have conducted the investigations have done so in order to disprove any claims of divine intervention. While scientists have wanted to have nothing to do with any explanation which might suggest supernatural intervention, or contradict their rational view of the world, the Church too has had its motives in attempting to belittle the experience of the stigmatists wherever possible. One reason it views claims of the miraculous and supernatural with extreme caution is, presumably, that it has not wished to yield any of its authority in religious matters to a 'hysterical' stigmatic. Yet despite all this predisposition to scepticism, and while self-mutilation and fraud are possible and probably have occurred, there is no doubt that cases of stigmatics have been and still are reported which can only be described as genuine.

But what is meant by genuine? Have the marks been divinely imprinted? Has God looked down on earth and spotted certain especially pious individuals to whom he wishes to give a sign of his particular favour? These are questions to be examined in due course. Initially however the term 'genuine' will be used to describe those cases where there is no evidence to cast doubt on a claim that the marks appeared spontaneously without any deliberate, conscious, physical act on behalf of the recipient.

In the first undisputed case, St Francis of Assisi received his marks in the course of a vision of a crucified seraph. St Francis was at the time fasting and concentrating intently on his prayers and meditations on the Gospel accounts of the Passion and suffering of Christ. He had journeyed under difficult conditions to Monte la Verna in central Italy and it was while he was on the mountain, away from his companions, that he had his vision. He saw a six-winged seraph, in the middle of which was the image of a man nailed to a cross. Subsequent paintings of the scene show five lines of force like thin beams of light etching the stigmata on the saint's hands, feet and side.

The story of his journey and his stigmatization has now become a legend. On his trip to the mountain it is said, amongst other things, that the saint found a previously unknown spring as a reward for a peasant who had lent him his mule. And at the foot of the last precipice, as the party rested under an oak tree, flocks of birds are said to have come to greet him. The moment of stigmatization came around 14th September 1224, the Feast of the Exultation of the Holy Cross. This somewhat minor festival was, in the thirteenth century, celebrated with considerable fervour. St Francis was at that time totally absorbed in a longing to suffer for and with Christ. After his vision of the seraph, Francis' companions, so reports go, witnessed the wound in their leader's side which appeared to have been slashed as if by a spear. It was bleeding profusely. There were also nail marks on his hands. In the days that followed, according to the account given by Thomas of Celano, his trousers and tunic were often soaked in blood.

Since St Francis first exhibited the marks, the stigmata, although rare, have held peculiar fascination. They are classified as one of the mystical phenomena and yet are unique in that regard in that they are an accepted sign of mysticism which can be witnessed by believers and non-believers alike. There is no mistaking the blood, there is no mistaking the scarring on the bodies of the stigmatics.

Some of the stigmatics of history have appeared to those around them to be so pious and holy that it was a relatively short time after their death that the Church decided to venerate or canonize them. Others, who have had the marks, have been notorious in other ways. They have been objects of intense curiosity, which they have encouraged. They have almost appeared to enjoy the attention.

The vast majority of cases have occurred at a time and in a place where, although remarkable, reports of stigmata could be absorbed into the culture. Of the 321 cases identified by the French medic Dr Imbert-Gourbeyre up until 1908, 229 cases had been reported from Italy. While his figures are not entirely reliable, sufficient credence can be given to them for such a bias in favour of one particular country to be seen as significant. When it is borne in mind that a further 70 cases originated from France, 47 from Spain and 13 from Portugal it will be seen that the Roman Catholic countries, mostly with a Latin and Mediterranean influence, have dominated the history of stigmata.

The history however of stigmata in the twentieth century shows a change in pattern. While Italy provides many examples, it does not dominate in quite the same way. There have been American cases, one in Australia, and of the known living stigmatics, three are British. The twentieth century too has seen stigmatics from Churches other than the Roman Catholic Church. At least three Anglicans have borne the marks in recent times.

It is interesting to note from Imbert-Gourbeyre's study that a significant proportion of cases are to be found amongst members of religious orders. Both the Dominicans and the Franciscans have provided over a hundred cases each, although until the twentieth century, very few priests could be included in this number.

One thing however which is very obvious from the study of the history of stigmata is that women outnumber men by a ratio of 7 to 1. The reason is not, in all probability, an obvious one. It would appear that it is not a simple case of women being more susceptible to whatever the factor might be that causes the stigmata. Indeed to understand why women have received the marks more often, and to understand why the phenomenon occurred for the first time in the thirteenth century, is to get close to a wider understanding of stigmata itself.

This book aims to explore these questions both through an examination of the lives of the stigmatics from history and through the evidence of living witnesses, especially those who have experienced the marks themselves or been close to those who have received them.

First however the question of authenticity must be examined. How do the stigmata fit into the modern scientific medical view of the world?

❖

A Medical View

For at least two hundred years members of the medical profession have had the opportunity to examine individual stigmatics. That the wounds have appeared in many people without any deliberate conscious physical intervention is now generally accepted. Indeed, in the case of Ethel Chapman, the wounds appeared while she was in hospital under constant medical supervision.

And for doctors to accept that such mysterious events do happen, does not require a difficult mental leap which might threaten their usual rationalism. For it has long been accepted by the medical profession that wounds can appear on the body which seem to have no external physical cause. Most of these do not have any religious connotation and are described as being of psychosomatic origin. It is accepted by secular observers and physicians that it is quite natural, if rare, for specific marks to appear on the body which are produced as a result of the unconscious working of the mind on the body.

It is generally accepted that emotional stress of various kinds can produce marks on the skin. At a very basic level blushing is an example. More complicated examples include such things as eczema. Yet marks can appear of a much more specific nature.

In the medical journal *The Lancet* of December 28th 1946 a case was described of a thirty-five-year-old man who, while under close observation in hospital, had produced wounds on his arms corresponding to the rope marks he had received nine years earlier when being forcibly restrained. The marks were clear indentations which also bled. His doctor concluded that there was no way to describe what he had seen as other than a 'genuine psychosomatic phenomenon'. When the marks had appeared the patient had seemed to be severely disturbed, reliving in his mind and in his actions the original experience which had caused the injuries.

The same doctor reported three other cases where similar symptoms had occurred. In one case a man who had relived the experience of being buried in a building following a flying-bomb explosion, reproduced the marks of the ankle and head injuries he had received at the time. It was reported that he was in acute pain for several hours during this episode.

In 1967 three doctors from Cleveland, Ohio published a report on the case of four women patients. They had all exhibited curious wounds which seemed to correspond to past injuries. They were interviewed extensively, kept under close observation to ensure that the wounds were not self-inflicted and questioned under hypnosis. In one case a woman, when hypnotized, had the suggestion made to her that she re-experience her original injury. Quite spontaneously her foot became painful and began to swell.

The expanded capabilities of the mind under hypnosis and the consequent effect on the body may not be unrelated to some aspects of the stigmatic condition. There is certainly the one case of a doctor suggesting to a hypnotized patient that she receive the marks, which she did accordingly. The doctor in question was a German medic, Dr Alfred Lechler, and his experiment was carried out in 1928 on a seriously disturbed patient he was treating. Whatever the ethics of his decision to experiment he was able to induce in her visions of crucifixion very similar to those reported by stigmatics and one of the most dramatic parts of his experiment he described in this way.

It was suggested to Elizabeth that a crown of thorns was put on her head and after an hour several red marks the size of a pea appeared on her forehead. In the middle of these marks red blood spots the size of pinheads appeared. During the following hours the blood spots increased and from several of them blood emerged. Some drops were large enough to roll down the forehead. During all that time Elizabeth complained of headache and a sensation of pinpricks. The continuous observation of the proceedings was done by me and the nurses. I myself could clearly see the emergence of the blood in several places.

There are various other, more ethical, reports of hypnosis having a profound effect on the skin, one of the most dramatic involving a cure for a persistent skin condition ichthyosiform erythrodermia. This report dates from 1951 and was reported in the *British Medical Journal*. It was suggested under hypnosis that a thick layer of unsightly skin on the patient's arm, which had stoutly resisted all other medical treatment, would disappear.

About five days later the horny layer softened, became friable and fell off . . . from a black and armour-like casing, the skin became pink and soft within a few days . . . at the end of ten days the arm was completely clear from shoulder to wrist.

Hypnosis aside, by 1989 some 71 cases had been described of spontaneous lesions for which there was no physical explanation and the term psychogenic purpura had been coined. It was noticed too that all the patients with such lesions, when examined, tended to share a similar personality profile. The general patient profile emerging was that of a woman with a disturbed or traumatic psychiatric history and a record of various kinds of spontaneous bleeding. Some of this bleeding had been from the nose, others had had to have internal gastro-intestinal bleeding treated and 25 had reported blood in the urine. Nearly all complained of severe headaches and there was a tendency amongst them to have had problems with their vision, periods of being unable to speak and faintness. One of the most interesting parallels involves hallucinations or, as in the case of stigmata, 'visions'. In one 1962 study of psychogenic purpura Dr David Agle and Dr Oscar Ratnoff reported the case of a patient who had hallucinations of her dead father and of another who talked of 'seeing gold' when she became angry. The same article which appeared in *Archives of Internal Medicine* talked of patients with masochistic character traits and a tendency to be able to endure illness and the pain of surgical procedures 'far beyond the limits set by a normally strong ego and more suggestive of actual enjoyment of the hardship'. Stigmatics too have talked of the rewards of their sufferings with Christ and many too in the twentieth century have undergone extensive surgery or hospitalization in addition to receiving their religious experiences.

The same article also raised as a final thought that it was 'tempting to inquire about the specific symbolism of purpura for our patients. For example, are these abreactions of previous real trauma or the beating fantasies of masochists?'

Of the 71 cases accumulated by Dr Ratnoff by 1989, 10 of the patients involved reported hallucinations and 29 were described as masochistic or martyristic.

In one of the modern cases of psychogenic purpura something very curious, indeed unique to such studies, occurred. The patient examined appeared to exhibit injuries which she herself had not originally received but had witnessed. She was hypnotized and asked to re-experience in her mind the traumatic events of the occasion when she had witnessed a neighbour being shot. She became tearful and began to writhe about in her chair. She spoke of the boy's screams and her own feelings of helplessness. It was suggested to her that she develop a mark on her lower right thigh similar to her neighbour's wounds. In the twenty-four hours following the trance she developed a mark around her left eye, but not her thigh. She said however that she felt as though she had been beaten up. The next day after a second spell of hypnosis and further suggestions she complained of a pinching feeling about her right knee and later in the day the area became red and swollen and within twenty-four hours a bruise occurred. A week later she complained that the lesion was increasingly painful and said that the blood had seeped through the skin. The wounds the woman re-created did not precisely correlate to what she had seen but they were unique in that her wounds appeared to be produced as an act of empathy.

Patients with this condition were predominantly but not exclusively women. In 1974 a case history was published by a team of doctors from the University of Rochester School of Medicine in New York of a fifty-three-year-old man of Italian extraction. He had had lesions which had appeared spontaneously. The doctors concluded that the pain was a symptom which had developed during a period of sustained psychological stress brought on by the death of his mother, marital problems and a heart attack.

While reporting what they had seen and accepting that the psychosomatic injuries occurred, the medical profession has, in the words of one doctor, 'no inkling how emotional pressures bring about these obvious organic results', and in the journal *Psychological Medicine* of 1978 one doctor wrote:

> We have little doubt that our own biases in this matter incline us to seek psycho-physiological explanations and to discard the more commonly accepted view that in most cases the lesions were fraudulent or self-induced.

At one time an attempt was made to suggest that psychogenic purpura was entirely a physical condition caused by patients reacting abnormally to their own blood. The condition was then described as autoerythrocyte sensitization. However when it was noticed that the patients all appeared to have a broadly similar psychological profile, the view was revised. Later it was noted that this profile also had many things in common with the personality profiles of certain contemporary stigmatics. However with the one exception of the woman who witnessed the shooting of a neighbour, the two conditions are very different. Psychogenic purpura recalls in a very physical sense a past trauma experienced by the patient, the sufferer him- or herself. In the stigmata, all recipients of the marks are acting out the wounds which appeared on someone else's body. They are suffering in empathy with Christ.

Drawing parallels between psychogenic purpura and stigmata suggests that a similar psychosomatic mechanism is involved in producing both sets of marks. At present there is no accepted medical model to explain how the marks appear psychosomatically, even though it is accepted that they do.

A second theory could be suggested which involves both internal and external factors, mental and physical processes. It is possible that the marks of stigmata appear as a result of unconscious physical intervention. There is a school of thought which proposes that the study of stigmatics is similar to a study of individuals with multiple personalities. This theory was examined by Ian Wilson in his book *The Bleeding Mind*.

The case for a link increases when we find that many of the ailments suffered by multiple personality patients are reminiscent of those we have come across in stigmatics . . . What is evident is that stigmata and multiple personality seem to be so closely linked that they could be two different aspects of the same phenomenon . . . In both we find the individual caught up in a flight from reality, on the one hand into a fantasy personality providing some form of release or escape from the constraints on the everyday self, and on the other into an established fantasy world of religious figures and a personal dramatization of the events surrounding the death of Jesus.

Patients with multiple personalities have, it seems, lived parallel lives. One self is often unaware of the others. To give an example, there was reportedly a case of a neat and conservative Georgia housewife who would unexpectedly snap into a personality who would speak coarsely and wear provocative dress.

The same woman, to quote Ian Wilson, 'found herself prey to some twenty invading personalities who would take her over in such a way she would be amnesic during those times they took charge. Different personalities even had different handwriting.'

Examining the meditations and prophetic writings of the Lincoln stigmatist Heather Woods, her handwriting, which was always done with her left hand even though she was right-handed, can be seen on occasions to vary from paragraph to paragraph. Up to three or four styles might be visible on one page. She talks of receiving messages from various sources ranging from sixteenth-century figures to one recently deceased Anglican evangelist.

If, as is the case with multiple personalities, one character does not recall what the other characters have said or done, could something similar happen to the stigmatist? That while he or she, in one personality is undergoing a vision which is later recalled by their normal self, another self might exist which physically makes marks on the body, which the normal self does not later recall having made. Thus the stigmatist, in his or her normal personality, would recall a vision and also find bodily marks but be unaware that he or she had made them. To the conscious normal personality the vision and the appearance of the marks would be linked and be attributed to one and the same cause. And given the extraordinary nature of the experience as perceived by the recipient that cause would be explained as mystical or divine.

Then, once the marks were established and known about, there might be a very understandable human temptation on that person to maintain the marks so as not to lose face or cease to be the centre of attention or devotion.

In saying all this it is not to suggest fraudulent intent. To the individual the experience would have been very real. It is only to suggest an alternative mechanism to the purely psychosomatic and does not in any way undermine the interest in the phenomenon or belittle the significance read into them by many witnesses.

One is not here examining mutually exclusive

explanations. Clearly in some cases of stigmata, and certainly in some recorded cases of psychogenic purpura, there is indisputable evidence that marks were the product of mind over matter. Take the case for instance of the man who produced rope wounds on his arms under medical observation: no ropes were involved to apply pressure to his skin and flesh.

Indeed if it can be argued that multiple personality disorder is involved in stigmata, and there is no firm evidence for such a theory, it would certainly not be the only mechanism. It might be involved in some cases but probably only a minority, leaving the psychosomatic route as being the favoured explanation in the majority of cases.

In medieval times, even marks which had been consciously produced would not necessarily have been dismissed as fraudulent. They would admittedly not have been interpreted as mystical marks but could certainly have been seen as evidence of genuine piety. It was well recognized that a person wishing to empathize with the passion of Christ might have consciously chosen the path of suffering and physical pain. Deliberate mortification of the flesh was not unusual. It was a regular form of penance to wear a hair shirt or to undergo flagellation.

Indeed in medieval times the first question put by witnesses on seeing a case of stigmata, would not necessarily have been, are these wounds physically made or otherwise? There was less of a clear cut division between the physical and the spiritual, between this world and the next. The evidence of the shared suffering with Christ would have been enough to inspire awe. Today however the question of physical involvement and physical intervention is the key one. If physical intervention is suggested then the marks are assumed to be fraudulent, or at least worthy of little note.

To explain away stigmata as merely a form of psychogenic purpura with religious overtones is to undervalue and underestimate the phenomenon. For while medical cases tend to attract little attention away from medical circles and be of little interest to anyone other than those directly concerned, stigmata rouses a whole range of emotions within the community in which it appears. In addition a variety of other mystical phenomena is frequently associated with stigmata and so whatever the medical similarities might be between psychogenic purpura and stigmata, stigmata needs to be examined within a much wider framework for it involves people asking of themselves certain essential religious questions and stimulates devotion, piety, hostility or rampant disbelief.

Before continuing down that road, however, mention should be made of a recent maverick theory published in the *Fortean Times* in 1993. It was the work of the writer Jim Schnabel who linked stigmata and mystical phenomena with a wide variety of other reported events including UFO abductions and spirit possession together with the medical condition of Munchausen's syndrome and Munchausen's syndrome by proxy. This all embracing idea included shamanism, bulimia and self-mortification.

In essence he suggested that all these conditions were to be found in similar personality types and involved the elevation of the lowliest members of society to positions of substantial power through a long experience of oppression or illness and a crisis involving possession or wounding by other worldly entities. The shamans, Schnabel pointed out, were often described as 'wounded healers' and the suggestion was made that to become wounded, shamans might deliberately expose themselves to suffering or fake the effects. He also pointed out that many of the phenomena associated with these activities were primarily the province of women or shaman who were themselves bisexual or transexual. These phenomena, it was pointed out, enabled practitioners to achieve ends which they could not secure more directly. They did so by capitalizing on their distress, making a special virtue of adversity and affliction. The practitioners were able to give their exhibitions of extraordinary powers more force by learning sleight of hand and other ways of tricking an audience. They also knew ways of elevating their consciousness to a genuinely altered state through eating hallucinatory substances, chanting rhythmically or undergoing pain and self-mutilation.

It is an appealing though highly speculative theory. It certainly fits the behaviour of a number of stigmatics and others the author categorizes as being of the same type, including Munchausen's patients who are people of low self-esteem who use pain and fake symptoms to attract attention to themselves.

THREE

Cases from the Past

In his Epistle to the Galatians (6:17), St Paul writes 'I bear in my body the marks of the Lord Jesus'. In the Greek the word he uses for the marks is 'stigmata' and he was describing marks such as would be made by piercing nails or a sharp instrument.

It is an open debate as to whether St Paul was speaking figuratively or was referring to wounds of punishment and suffering he himself had endured and was through these wounds allying himself with Christ. Or is it possible that his marks, stigmata, were similar to those which were to appear twelve hundred years later as a rare but regular feature of mysticism and believed to be of supernatural and divine origin?

A character profile of St Paul, drawn from what information is available from his letters and from the Acts of the Apostles, would suggest that he had some of the characteristics of the later stigmatists. At the time of his conversion he had a dramatic vision and heard a voice. Yet one would suppose that if he had had the stigmata physically and spontaneously this would have been acknowledged in other writings or traditions, and the stigmata as a phenomenon of Christian piety would have become the unusual but established phenomenon it is, somewhat earlier in the history of Christendom.

As it was, it was nearly twelve centuries after St Paul that the stigmata were next reported. Arguably the very first case was in Oxford where in 1222 a man was imprisoned after claiming that he carried on his body the five wounds of crucifixion. Describing events, the monk Thomas Wykes suggested that in this case the marks were self-inflicted.

> There was presented . . . a layman, whose madness was such that he passed himself to be crucified, to the dishonour of the crucified one, declaring that he was the son of God and the redeemer of the world. He was incarcerated . . . for the rest of his life and fed only on hard bread and water.

It is not in character for a stigmatist to make a declaration that he is the son of God. Thomas Wykes' observation is probably correct that these marks were self-inflicted. Although it is possible that they could have been spontaneously produced and those who saw the marks could only deduce that they must have been self-inflicted. What is significant is that the man's experience is an indication of a new importance being given at that period to the contemplation of the sufferings of Christ. This was a general mood which grew in strength through that period, partly as a reaction by certain pious people against certain excesses and corruption in the Church. This contemplation of suffering took varying forms ranging from a renewed interest in devotion to the body of Christ through, in its extreme form, to the activities of people like the French nobleman Robert Carr, Marquis of Montferrard who died in 1234. For many years this devout gentleman had, amongst other penances, pierced his flesh every Friday with nails in order to share the suffering of Christ.

Yet by the time of the death of the Marquis of Montferrard an undisputed case of the stigmata had introduced the phenomenon to the Christian world. This was the case of St Francis of Assisi.

St Francis is one of the great Christian saints whose life and witness is well known. The story of his irresponsible youth, his conversion to the aesthetic life, his empathy with the natural world and his founding of one of the major monastic orders is familiar and often told. However it was only two years before his death, when his reputation was well established, that he received the marks which were to confirm to many Christians his particular sanctity. Interestingly the marks he received were not wounds which bled but impressions of the heads of the nails, round and black and standing clear from the flesh.

The 'miracle' of St Francis' stigmatization was described, shortly after the death of the saint, by Brother Elias in a letter sent to the Provincial of France.

I announce to you a new miracle. From the beginning of ages there has not been heard so great a wonder, save only in the son of God, who is Christ our God. For, a long while before his death, our Father and Brother appeared crucified, bearing in his body the five wounds which are verily the stigmata of the Christ; for his hands and feet had as it were piercings made by nails fixed in from above and below, which laid open the scars and had the black appearance of nails; while his side appeared to have been lanced, and blood often trickled there from.

Another contemporary account was written by Francis' companion Brother Leo.

> The blessed Francis, two years before his death, kept a Lent in the hermitage of the Alverna in honour of the Blessed Virgin Mary, mother of God, and Blessed Michael the Archangel, from the Feast of the Assumption of St Mary the Virgin to the Feast of St Michael in September. And the hand of the Lord was laid upon him. After the vision and speech he had of a seraph, and the impression in his body of the Stigmata of Christ, he made these praises . . . giving thanks to God for the favour that had been conferred on him.

That St Francis received his marks in this way has been disputed. In a monograph published in 1910, Dr J. Merkt of Tübingen University claimed that the marks did not date back to the vision of the seraph but appeared only a few weeks before his death. Also Dr Merkt maintained, to quote the twentieth-century Jesuit scholar Father Herbert Thurston's summary:

> The wounds were little more than discolourations or abrasions of the skin which could easily have been

produced and probably were produced, by purely pathological conditions, given a subject whose thoughts were almost uninterruptedly concentrated upon the marks of our Saviour's Passion.

Dr Merkt did not however dispute that at his death St Francis did in fact display the marks, only the timing and circumstances of their arrival did he question.

Shortly after the death of St Francis a second, less famous case of stigmata occurred at Hascha in Frisia. In 1231 a Praemonstratensian monk, Brother Dodo, was killed when the wall of an old ruin fell upon him. For the five years before he had led a solitary life and when his body was removed from the rubble it was discovered that there were open wounds in his hands and feet and in his right side corresponding to the five wounds of crucifixion. That he had been carrying such marks in his lifetime had been unknown and thus it is not possible to say if Brother Dodo's marks were stigmata, similar to those of St Francis, or the result of wounds which were self-inflicted by the hermit as part of his devotions to the Passion.

As the thirteenth century progressed the instances of stigmata increased. In the century following the death of St Francis more than twenty cases were reported.

Some time before 1237 the Blessed Helen, a Dominican sister at a convent in Veszprim in Hungary, received a mark in her right hand on the Feast of St Francis and later received the wound in her side. In 1268 St Christina of Stommeln received wounds in her hands, feet, on her forehead and in her side. She attempted to keep them secret, but not entirely successfully. Stories that her wounds bled every Easter quickly spread. Stories also circulated that St Christina was harassed by terrifying demonic experiences. She was seen to be hurled against a wall by an unseen power and, according to one report 'be spattered and polluted with deluges of indescribable filth'. She also experienced religious raptures and divine ecstasies and on Whit Sunday 1268, after making her communion, she is said to have remained motionless for many hours, caught up in a religious trance. Her life was carefully documented by her parish priest and she was described as a 'holy woman and a true spouse of Christ'.

Another stigmatic of the thirteenth century who experienced ecstasies, the Blessed Angela of Foligno near Assisi, was also the first stigmatic who was able, it was claimed, to live for long periods of time without food. In her case twelve years. She was a widow who had sold everything she owned to join the Third Order of St Francis. The Blessed Angela was also the author of a famous set of revelations and her reputation is well established as one of the classic mystics of medieval times. She was also subjected to what were described as diabolic temptations. Another of her experiences which was later to be repeated by other women stigmatics involved a vision in which she felt herself being given the Christ child to hold.

In examining medieval cases it is sometimes difficult to distinguish between cases of stigmata which appeared spontaneously and those which were clearly induced by physical means. It was the mystical consequences which were of far more interest to the medieval onlooker. Whereas today such a distinction is all important to the modern rational mind, as marks which are consciously self-produced are dismissed as fraudulent, while those which may be supposed to be spontaneous are concluded to be genuine.

The case of Lukardis of Oberweimar illustrates the medieval approach. She was born around 1276 and died at the age of thrity-three. An anonymous biographer recorded her mystical life which was made up of ecstatic experiences and stigmatization from an early age. Yet she was also known to have involved herself in practices of self-mutilation and her biographer described how, as she recalled in her mind the hammering of nails into Christ's hands, she repeated the action physically.

For again and again with her middle finger she would strike violently the place of the wounds in each palm; and then at once drawing back her hand a couple of feet she delivered another fierce blow in the same spot, the tip of her finger seeming somehow to be pointed like a nail. Indeed though it appeared a finger to sight and touch, neither flesh nor bone could be felt in it and those who had handled it declared that it had the hardness of a piece of metal. When she struck herself in that way there was a sound like the ring of a hammer falling on the head of a nail or on an anvil. On one occasion a person in authority thinking this kind of blow was a sham or a mere trick, in order to find out the truth put his hand in the way. But when she had struck but once he hastily drew back his hand, declaring that if he had waited for a second blow he would have lost the use of it for ever. With the same finger, at the hour of Sext and again at None, the servant of God used to strike herself violently on the breast where the wound came. The noise that she made was so great that it echoed through the whole convent, and so exactly did she keep to the hours of Sext and None in this practice that the nuns found the sound more trustworthy than the clock . . . Furthermore, it should be noted that the Servant of God, before the stigmata appeared, endeavoured out of her great longing, to open the places of the wounds in her feet by boring them, as it were, with her big toe.

Lukardis' biographer was not in any way intending to suggest that she was not the recipient of genuine wounds. For having described her strange practices, which had been going on for two years before the stigmata showed, he then describes the mystic's nocturnal vision during which the stigmata were impressed upon her.

It is said that a 'beautiful and delicate youth appeared to her and pressed his right hand against her right hand saying, ''I wish thee to suffer along with me.'' To this she gave consent and immediately a wound was formed on her right hand.'

Her biographer then relates how Lukardis was embarrassed by her marks and initially hid them from view by wearing gloves. The wounds, as has happened with so many other stigmatics, bled regularly on Fridays.

It soon became apparent that, despite the early stigmatics having been men, it was predominately to be women who were to receive the marks in the first centuries of the phenomenon. A pattern of behaviour also became established. Many of those who received the wounds were members of religious orders and also exhibited a wide range of symptoms ranging from what have been described as the 'mystical' to the 'hysterical'. Many achieved reputations for their holiness and were later to be canonized. In this book there is only space to mention a few of the most famous or infamous instances of the stigmata appearing.

St Catherine of Siena was born in 1347 and is one of a number of stigmatics who died at the significant age of thirty-three years, the age at which it is believed Christ died on the cross. She first felt the pain of Christ's suffering in her own body at the age of twenty-six and two years later, it is said, received five visible wounds. She also experienced the symptom of being unable or unwilling to eat. She went, it is said, for eight years without taking any food or liquid other than the Blessed Sacrament.

There were also reports of St Catherine levitating and Father Herbert Thurston wrote, 'the evidence for her levitations seems quite overwhelming'. After her death Catherine's body, as in the case of a number of other stigmatics, is said not to have decomposed in the normal way and centuries later the stigmata were traceable on Catherine's body by a transparency in the tissues, although in her lifetime St Catherine had prayed that her marks should not be conspicuous.

The saint is also said to have experienced another phenomenon closely akin to stigmatization in which it is said her soul entered a form of mystic espousal with Christ. She is said, in 1367, to have had a vision in which she saw

Jesus and Mary, St John the Evangelist, St Paul and St Dominic, the founder of her order. During the vision Mary took Catherine's right hand and held it out to her son who placed a ring of gold and diamonds on her finger with the words 'receive this ring as a pledge and testimony that you are mine and will be mine for ever'.

After the vision, Catherine said that she always saw the ring on her finger, although it was invisible to others. After her death her ring finger was kept as a relic. Amongst other stories recounted about St Catherine is that as she was being given Holy Communion the priest felt the Host become agitated and fly, as if of its own volition, from his fingers into her mouth.

And yet more curious stories are told about Catherine which are not unique to her but shared by others who have had the marks of the cross. One legend which has been told is of her immunity to fire. In her *Life of St Catherine*, Mother Francis Raphael recounts the story of how Catherine fell forward into a fire in the kitchen during a religious ecstasy. The fire was large and fierce, but when Catherine was pulled out of the smoking embers it was found 'she had received no injury either in her person or even her clothes and yet it was a great fire and she a long time in it'.

Moving on 300 years to the story of another woman later to be canonized for her piety, the story of Catherine is echoed by that of St Veronica Giuliani, who at the age of thirty-seven received the stigmata in hands, side and feet. The marks appeared in the course of a long period of ecstasy on April 5th 1697. Veronica kept a journal and tells of the whole experience. Earlier on Easter Day in 1694 she had become espoused to Jesus in the course of a vision, and in the course of her ecstatic vision three years later she saw the Virgin Mary say to her son, Christ, 'let thy bride be crucified with thee'.

Veronica wrote an account of what followed which closely parallels the experience of St Francis of Assisi.

In an instant I saw five brilliant rays of light dart forth from the Five Sacred Wounds, and all seemed to concentrate their force upon me. And I saw that these rays became small flames of burning fire. Four of them appeared in the form of great pointed nails, whilst the fifth was a spear-head of gleaming gold, all a quiver as thrice heated hot. And this, a levin flash, lancing upon me, pierced my heart through and my feet. I felt a fearful agony of pain, but with the pain I clearly saw and was conscious that I was wholly transformed into God. When I had been thus wounded, in my heart, in my hands and feet, the rays of light gleaming with a new radiance shot back to the Crucifix, and illumed the gashed side, the hands and feet of Him who was hanging there. Thus My Lord and My God espoused me, and gave me in charge to His Most Holy Mother for ever and ever, and bade my Guardian Angel watch over me, for He was jealous of His honour, and then thus He spake to me: 'I am Thine, I give Myself wholly unto thee. Ask whatsoever thou wilt, it shall be granted thee.' I made reply: 'Beloved, only one thing I ask, never to be separated from Thee.' And then in a twinkling all vanished away.

When I came to myself I found that I was kneeling

with my arms wide outspread, benumbed and sore
cramped, and my heart, my hands and my feet burned
and throbbed with great pain. I felt that my side was
gashed open and welled and bubbled with blood. I
tried to open my habit and see the wound, but I could
not because of the wounds in both my hands. After
a while, with much suffering, I succeeded in loosing
my habit, and I then saw that the wound in my side
purled forth with water and blood.

It was Veronica's wish that the marks would not be
generally seen. However they remained visible until the
year 1700, in fulfilment of a promise from Jesus given in
a vision that the marks would only last three years. After
that date only the bleeding side remained. Veronica was
one of those stigmatics whose heart was examined after
death and found, so it is said, to have been marked in a
way which had been foreseen during her lifetime. Veronica
had told her confessor that her heart would bear images
of various kinds, including a cross, a crown of thorns and
a chalice. Thirty hours after her death professors of
medicine and surgery conducted a postmortem
examination and said that on her heart were imprints
similar to those which Veronica had visualized and drawn
when she was still alive. The postmortem also revealed 'a
very considerable curvature of the right shoulder, which
bent the very bone just as the weight of a heavy cross might
have done'. This latter sentence might indicate a certain
religious imagination on behalf of the examining doctors,
and the surgeon who performed the autopsy was quite clear
in his evidence that:

if this curvature had occurred by natural means it would have prevented her moving her arm, but I have myself frequently seen Sister Veronica during her last illness move her right arm without the least difficulty.

As for the marks seen on her heart it could also be argued that those who interpreted them did not do so with entirely open minds in that they were probably looking for the specific signs Veronica had previously drawn. All hearts will carry a profusion of marks made up from the organs, blood vessels and muscles, and where there is a willing imagination these marks can presumably be interpreted in any way required.

St Veronica was also said during her ecstasies to have emitted the sweet odour of sanctity around her and claims too were made that she had levitated. In one report it is claimed she had defied gravity and 'risen to the tree-tops'. While cases of levitation are rare, reports of a sweet perfumed smell associated with mystics and stigmatics are more common. Indeed the odour of sanctity predates the stigmata by one thousand years. In A.D. 155 the Christians of Smyrna described the attempted execution by burning of St Polycarp. Initially the fires failed to harm the bishop and witnesses later described how at the time they watched Polycarp surrounded by flames but unharmed and how they perceived 'such a fragrant smell, as if it were the wafted odour of frankincense or some other precious spice'. In the end the bishop was despatched by an executioner with a dagger.

In the words of Father Herbert Thurston, 'already in

the second century the idea was familiar throughout the Christian world that high virtue was in some cases miraculously associated with fragrance of body'.

Not surprisingly the stigmatized mystics became associated with this sweet heavenly smell. This association has persisted to this century and it is said frequently of Padre Pio that his spiritual presence could be detected by a smell as if of scented roses.

Two features of stigmata which have now been generally overlooked or under-appreciated are its geographical distribution and social context. While many cases have occurred to individuals in isolation, some living the lives of hermits or recluses, there have been instances where whole communities seem to have been caught up in a collective piety and more than one person has been found to be carrying the marks. Most examinations of stigmata to date have examined the phenomenon from the individual's point of view. Stigmatics have either, it is said, received their marks from God, or from their own reaction to a religious experience. However by looking at the way in which the marks have emerged in geographical clusters, it could be suggested that some cases are better examined in the following way: that certain individuals within a community, perhaps those with personalities best suited to producing psychosomatic symptoms, have received the marks on behalf of their community. They are, as it were, that community's icon. Where more than one person exists with a propensity to psychosomatic symptoms, more than one case of stigmata is reported. For this to happen of course the community itself needs to be going through some form of collective religious experience or heightened spiritual awareness.

In the 1830s in the Tyrol three cases were reported within a year of each other, at a time when the Tyrolean people were undergoing a period of religious revival. The best known case was that of Maria de Moerl, a Franciscan tertiary who in the late autumn of 1833 received the five bleeding wounds. She was counselled to keep her experience a secret as far as possible, and the secret was kept until the day of the Corpus Christi procession through the streets of Kaldern in 1834.

In his book *The Physical Phenomena of Mysticism*, Montigue Summers wrote:

It so happened that from the windows of the Moerl house, and from Maria's bedroom, an excellent view could be obtained of the procession with its groups of winged angels and tableaux of Saints and seraphim. It was high holiday throughout the district. Friends and neighbours crowded the house of the Moerls. Maria's room, as she lay in bed, was full of young girls, laughing, talking, jostling for a place. As the Blessed Sacrament beneath its canopy, in fumes of frankincense, surrounded by myriad tapers, passed the window, one of the company in the room glanced round saying 'Poor Maria! She can't see the—' The sentence was broken by a cry. Maria had fallen into ecstasy. She was levitated from the bed, and transfigured with an angelic beauty, radiant as a celestial spirit, her arms extended, her feet not touching the bed, and the stigmata shining with a clear crystal light. All witnessed the phenomenon, which could no longer be kept concealed.

The countryside rang with the story. Groups of pilgrims began to pour into Kaldern. From near and far they came in orderly procession, often led by the parish priest. It was estimated that between the end of July and the 15th September more than forty thousand persons, rich and poor, peer and peasant, had palmered it to Kaldern.

At almost exactly the same time at Capriana in the Tyrol, a second case of stigmata emerged involving a miller's daughter, Domenica Lazzari. Her mystic experiences started shortly before Maria de Moerl's experiences became public knowledge. Domenica Lazzari's wounds were said to have bled every Friday from the time of the first appearance through to her death in 1848, at the age of thirty-three. Several witnesses described the wounds as going right through the palms of her hands. In addition to the five wounds she received the marks of the crown of thorns, when, during the night, as she said, 'a very beautiful lady came to my bedside and set a crown upon my head'. Again like many of the stigmatists of the centuries before, Domenica lived without food, only taking Holy Communion. Indeed it is said of her that she was hypersensitive to the presence of food.

According to Father Thurston no case is better attested than that of Domenica Lazzari.

The witnesses were men of high position, quite independent of each other, and their reports, which are in absolute accord regarding the main features of the case, cover a period of more than ten years. Still, the medical history of Domenica is a very curious one.

At the age of thirteen, shortly after her father's death, when she is said to have wept continuously for four days and four nights and eaten nothing in that time, she became seriously ill with a condition which her doctor described as 'hysteria marked by violent convulsions'. At the age of eighteen she had an unspecified terrifying experience, spending a night alone in a mill and nine days later was seized 'with a sort of cataleptic attack . . . and from that time forward she seems hardly to have left her bed until her death in 1848'. During that time she was hypersensitive to light, touch, heat and food.

In January 1837 the stigmata became visible and her face was often covered with a mask of blood trickling from the circlet of punctures representing the crown of thorns.

One witness to her suffering, which it appeared was extreme and almost continuous, was Lord Shrewsbury. He saw the wounds in her hands and feet and made this observation.

> Instead of taking its natural course, the blood flowed upwards over the toes, as it would do were she suspended on the cross.

This observation that the blood flow from Domenica's wounds appeared to contradict the law of gravity is not unique and in one of the most recent cases of stigmata, that of the American priest Father Jim Bruse, a similar flow of blood has been reported. Domenica is also reported to have spent long periods raining blows upon herself with such vigour that her 'gums were badly cut and her mouth was filled with blood'.

The third stigmatic of that period living in the Tyrol was born shortly after Domenica. Less has been written about her case, but Crescentia Nierklutsch was of the same generation and background as the other two Tyrolean stigmatics and would have been equally caught up in the religious atmosphere of the time.

A roll call of the stigmatics of the last two centuries includes a number of individuals who have received considerable local and in some cases worldwide fame or notoriety. One of these was Anne Catherine Emmerich, an Augustinian nun from near Westphalia in West Germany. She received the wounds in 1812, including one in her side shaped like the crucifix in the church she had known at Coesfeld when a child. Her experience lends support to the suggestion that the form in which wounds appear, and the details related about associated visions, can often be traced to, and is probably determined by, religious images with which the stigmatic has been familiar. Thus wounds have appeared, as in the case of Father Jim Bruse and others, of nailmarks in the wrists, only in the century or so since photographic techniques revealed the wounds so positioned in the Turin Shroud. Also in the case of Ethel Chapman, another twentieth-century stigmatic, her wounds and her visions corresponded to the illustrations in her Bible.

Many people who read the story of Anne Catherine Emmerich were however mystified as to how she had had access to some of the detail in her very vivid visions. She was described by Monsignor Albert Farges, in his *Treatise on Mystical Theology* published in 1926, as:

> An unlettered peasant who had never left her native village yet could see in her imagination the travels of the saviour through Palestine and describe its geography with exactitude, with its rivers, its mountains, its forests and its towns, with their inhabitants, their costume, their manners and customs, all these images are evidently transcendental and supernatural.

Mgr Farges was evidently very impressed by this, as were many contemporary witnesses, but appeared to make no attempt to investigate the claim that she was indeed uneducated. Investigations were made, however, by a sceptical local physician as to the genuineness of the marks themselves. In 1813 a team of doctors did however keep her under observation and reported back that during that time there had been no physical interference with her wounds. This would of course be consistent with a psychosomatic explanation of her experience, but leaves her mystical insight unexplained. As a nun she would have had access to many religious images, but these would not have explained her remarkable knowledge of far away places. One explanation perhaps lies in the fact that her visions were recounted to and recorded by someone who clearly had a much wider knowledge of the world. How much the accounts of Anne Catherine's visions taken down by the poet, Clemens Brentano, were coloured, consciously or unconsciously, by his knowledge and experience one cannot judge at this distance. It is known that taking notes from her was not easy as sometimes it was difficult to induce her to continue with a story, yet Brentano's four published volumes of the nun's insights contain the most elaborate detail about the Last Supper, the palace of Pilate, the burial of Jesus in the tomb, little of which detail appears in the Gospel accounts.

Anne Catherine Emmerich was yet another of the stigmatics to fast and to find it difficult to eat. When required by a religious superior to attempt to eat, the result is said to have been uncomfortable and painful. She exhibited symptoms similar to those patients suffering from anorexia who refuse food. Father Thurston in reviewing the experiences of Anne Catherine, St Catherine of Siena, Louise Lateau and Domenica Lazzari writes:

> Just as I should like to hear of a stigmatic who had no bad family history, and had always herself been a thoroughly healthy subject free from neuroses of any kind, so in the considerable list of those holy people who are reported to have lived for long periods with no other nourishment but the Blessed Sacrament, one looks, but looks in vain, for the name of one who was free from strange previous inhibitions in the matter of diet and whom the neuropath specialist would have pronounced to be perfectly sound and normal.

The most bizarre of the stigmatics of modern times could certainly have been included within Father Thurston's description. Therese Neumann was born in 1898 in Konnersreuth in Bavaria and was the

eldest daughter of a tailor. Her early history tells of
attempted rape and serious spinal and head injuries
and by 1919 she was blind and prone to alarming
fits. For four years she remained in a serious
condition with a paralysis of her left side and being
unable to speak. The story goes that in April 1923
she recovered her sight miraculously, announcing
that she could now see her brothers and sisters. Two
years later on the day of the canonization of Saint
Therese of Lisieux, Therese Neumann recovered
from her physical paralysis and announced that she
would now be able to get up and walk. This she did
and over the next weeks her strength gradually
returned. It was in 1926, however, that the
miraculous healings became a mystical event. She had
a vision of Christ at the Mount of Olives and she
had a pain in her side and felt blood trickling from
it. Later she found a wound had indeed opened up
in her side, and on Good Friday that year Therese
described seeing and living through Christ's entire
Passion. Nail wounds on her hands and feet also
appeared. The wounds remained with her until her
death in 1962. She also from that time refrained from
eating and became an object of considerable curiosity
and attention. There is one celebrated photograph
of her lying in a blood-soaked bed with blood
streaming from her eyes and hands. In her time
Therese Neumann was subjected to many
investigations, particularly to examine that which
could be most easily measured, her intake of food.
The results of some of these investigations have

aroused suspicions that Therese Neumann was not all she seemed or claimed to be. An analysis of urine output over a three-week period during which she was under constant observation suggests that during that time she was indeed fasting, but that once the twenty-four hour observations were eased her urine specimen suggested that she in some way found access to food and drink. She was however never caught in the act and no proof of fraud has ever been produced. It might be the case that her initial experiences and ability to survive on very little food were genuine, but that Therese Neumann extended the symptoms of her mysticism by physical means in order to retain her position as the centre of attention.

One of the first experiences of the stigmata to be claimed outside the Roman Catholic Church involves a British woman, Dorothy Kerin. She was the founder of the Burrswood Fellowship and Healing Ministry. She was born in 1889 and lived until 1963 and her mystical experiences began, like those of Therese Neumann, with a period in which she was deaf, blind and semi-conscious. Her family and friends expected her to die and gathered at her bedside at their home in Herne Hill, London, but were amazed when she confounded all predictions and raised herself, stood up and declared that she was healed. In a booklet entitled *London's Modern Miracle* the Rev. J. L. Thompson described the events of that Sunday evening.

The doctor had said she could not live until the morning. He had kept her alive for six weeks by means of brandy and opium and starch. During the last fortnight she had lain like a log of wood, and never moved her position in the bed, and was now blind and deaf, and for the most part unconscious. She had been attended by eight and twenty doctors, and had been sent home from an Incurable Home in an ambulance with only a week to live. She had been five years confined to her bed, and had been turned out of five hospitals – incurable.

Such was her condition, and now the end had come. About half past nine on Sunday evening, as mother and friends stood watching, she seemed to breathe her last. Anyhow, for eight minutes her lungs ceased to breathe, and her heart ceased to beat, and they deemed her dead. But just at this juncture, Dorothy tells us SOMEONE called her by name, three times distinctly, and she replied, 'Yes I am listening, who is it?' And He said, 'Listen!', and she felt two warm hands take hold of hers. A beautiful Light then flashed over the screen and came right over the bed. In the midst of the Light stood the Angel of the Lord, who, still holding her hands in His and lifting them up to her eyes and touching her ears, said, 'Dorothy, YOUR SUFFERINGS ARE OVER, GET UP AND WALK.'

She then opened her eyes and sat up, greatly wondering to see so many friends around her bed, to whom she said, 'I am well now! I want my dressing gown. I want to walk.' Of course her request was unheeded, and she began to get up without it, when her mother came and held her down, saying,

'No, Dorothy, you will fall, you must not get up!'
While thus held, the Angel again the second time
said, 'Get up and walk!' Dorothy then appealed to
her mother asking her if she did not hear, on which
she then relaxed her hold on her, and someone
suggested that the dressing gown should be given her
just to gratify her and convince her that she could
not walk.

Just then a part of the beautiful Light, seen only
by Dorothy, came and stood at the right hand side
of her bed. Then with eyes and ears opened, and
strength imparted to every limb, she threw off the
bed clothes from her, and stepped on to the floor,
placing her hand upon the Light that was to lead her.

The Light then moved forward, and she followed
saying to her friends, 'I am following the Light.' It
led her straight out of the room, through a passage
into a room where she expected to find her
stepfather, who, however, was not there. The Light
then led her into another room, where she found
him, and in the joy of her restoration she threw her
arms around his neck and kissed him.

The Light then led her back again to her own
room, where she found the whole company shaking
and trembling with fear! Her stepfather, who was
following her, then fell upon the floor, and began
to cry – in the attitude of prayer.

In the midst of this fear and amazement, Dorothy
seated herself saying, 'I cannot understand why you
are all so FRIGHTENED! I AM QUITE WELL.
Indeed, I feel as though I should like some supper!'

The account suggests that Dorothy, like other stigmatics before and since, was someone whose body and mind were closely linked. Indeed the very sort of person to whom a psychosomatic symptom like the stigmata could appear. And as in the cases of others who have received the marks it was some time after her initial 'healing', and once she had become established as a focus of awe in the community, that her stigmatization took place. Three years after her recovery she had a series of experiences which involved considerable pain and distress. During one she believed she had had a confrontation with the Devil 'in the form of a beautiful angel but with baleful eyes that held in them all the powers of evil'. Dorothy also experienced pains in the heart but her spiritual adviser felt that they were supernatural pains.

In the words of her biographer Dorothy Arnold:

> He noticed she appeared to have great pain in her left hand which she opened and shut constantly, while plucking the bed clothes with it. He saw a red spot gradually appear on the back of it.
>
> Later that same evening, he found her in a great state of distress. She said to him, showing him the palm of her left hand in which a wound was clearly visible, 'Do you think the Devil could have done this?' He replied, 'No, certainly not.' 'But,' she said, 'I am so wicked, God could not have done it. And if He had, surely He would have done it in both my hands. Do pray that it may go; not the pain, but the mark. I could not bear anyone to see it.' He replied he was sure it was the doing of our Lord, and

that she must be thankful, and that we had no right to say to our Lord what He must or must not do. This comforted her, and she eventually went into a deep sleep. He questioned her as to whether she had any idea of what it might be, and found that she had not and thought the Stigmata were always invisible. Before she fell asleep, she asked him to pray that the Stigmata might be removed in the night, not because she wanted to be rid of the pain, for she said she never wanted to lose that, but because she could not bear it to be seen. He prayed as she had asked him to do, but he also prayed that if it were God's Will the Stigmata might be given also in the right hand, so as to reassure her.

The next afternoon, December 9th, Dorothy received the Wound in her side. She was kneeling in front of the Crucifix kissing its Feet, when, preceded by a pain worse than on the previous occasion, she felt two stabs, as if a knife were being driven into her side. She collapsed in an agony of suffering, and when she came to herself she found the Wound in her right hand had also appeared.

On the following day, Saturday, December 10th, she was given the Wounds in her feet. In both her feet there appeared a round red mark on the instep . . . Her hand when she woke on the first occasion was full of blood, which vanished though she did not wash it. There remained a mark on the back of the hand like the head of a flat triangular nail; and on the palm a round wound that was bloodless.

Dorothy Kerin is best remembered for her healing ministry and was not a focus of attention solely because of her stigmata. Indeed she was famed initially for her miraculous recovery before any suggestion of mystical gifts. Her experiences however as a stigmatic were consistent with those of many others. She was able, it is reported, to consciously leave her physical body when at prayer at night to minister to the suffering of those for whom she was praying. And according to Dorothy Arnold 'many people told of their awareness of her healing ministrations despite the separation in space'. She talked too of religious ecstasies and of two visions in which she experienced the feeling of holding the Christ child in her arms.

Dorothy Kerin was not the first English example of a stigmatic. In the nineteenth century there was the case of Teresa Higginson who, while living in Bootle in Liverpool in the early 1880s, alarmed her neighbours by her repeated re-enactment of Christ's Passion. Some years earlier she had had ecstatic experiences and the stigmata appeared on her body at Easter time in 1874. Teresa Higginson had much in common and lived at the same time as Louise Lateau. Both had experienced traumatic injuries as children. In the case of Teresa she had thrown herself into a saw pit after the death of a younger brother and Louise was gored by a bull, or possibly injured by being trodden on by a cow, at the age of eleven. They were both objects of curiosity about the same time in the 1870s, both had religious ecstasies, were reluctant to eat and both considered to be either impostors or mentally unstable. While there is no conclusive proof of fraud, at the same time the lives of the two women were so bizarre, it is just as hard to contemplate that either woman was in receipt of gifts from God. Teresa Higginson for instance is said to have never slept and was subject to trances which appeared to serve her in place of sleep.

This has necessarily been a look at only a few of the key cases of stigmata, but even from them a pattern of experience and characteristics emerges. Around fifty cases have been reported and examined in detail by objective observers, with a further three hundred having been identified, although in some instances the three hundred have included cases of pious individuals reporting pain in hands, feet and side but producing no marks. These have been the invisible stigmata which some witnesses have believed to be genuine examples of suffering in empathy with Christ, but without external evidence it is difficult to include them in the same category as the visible marks.

Inevitably there must be some cases of stigmata which have occurred which have not been reported widely, or indeed reported at all, although it seems hard to imagine how a conspicuous set of marks can be kept secret by a recipient, especially if they survive on the body for any length of time and are present at death.

FOUR

Cases from the Present

The annals of medieval history are full of stories of curious and extravagant religious piety. There are tales of saints defying gravity and rising up into the air at times of religious ecstasy. Reports have been handed down of the remains of holy people staying supple and undecomposed after death. Saints have been said to exude a mysterious sweet perfume, the odour of sanctity. Indeed there is no shortage of extraordinary mystical phenomena associated with outstanding holy men and women of the past. Few of these reports satisfy the modern reader. They are not seen to be written by impartial observers and are thought to have been exaggerated over time. When no first-hand witnesses are available to be cross-questioned and when few original documents remain intact, it is impossible to verify the stories handed down from another age.

These reports however grow in credibility when compared with reports of similar modern events. Patterns of behaviour emerge. In most cases it is unlikely that those coming later knew enough about the past to be able to mimic the events of centuries before. Yet these modern cases exhibit many of the characteristics of the mystical events reported from times long ago. And these modern cases can be far more rigorously examined. Contemporary phenomena, however strange and improbable sounding, are more easy to verify.

One of the most closely documented cases of recent years has been that of Heather Woods, a forty-three-year-old widow living in Lincoln. Her wounds were captured on video on Good Friday 1993 and photographs were taken by her spiritual adviser at every key moment of her experience.

Heather is a deacon in a small episcopal Church which traces its roots back to pre-Roman Christianity in Britain and today has links with the Orthodox tradition. Heather's experience of receiving the marks is particularly rare because of this Orthodox connection. Nevertheless her experience is consistent with that of many other stigmatics. She has received wounds on her feet and hands, a crescent-shaped red mark on her right side and twice a vivid cross has appeared on her forehead.

Her marks first appeared in May 1992 and the first sign was an itching of her left hand. Something akin to a blister appeared on her hand with a halo-shaped mark around it. Over a period of a few days her right hand and her feet were similarly marked and, at their most active, the wounds have been the size of an old ten pence piece and have seeped blood and clear fluid. They have not taken the form of indentations but round flat areas of tender scarred skin.

Heather has a history of illness and has undergone surgery on many occasions. In the February before the stigmata appeared she was a patient in a hospice and her family and doctors expected her only to live for a few days.

However she had an experience which convinced her that she would not die on that occasion and before long would be able to discharge herself from the hospice. What she describes as a 'rather cryptic prayer' came into her mind. It was such a positive experience for her that she was convinced from that moment her strength would begin to return. This is indeed what happened.

The arrival of the marks on her hands coincided with her first experience of what she believes to be mystical writing and drawing. She received what she describes as spiritual messages which she wrote rapidly on whatever paper was to hand, little aware, she says, of what she was writing. Over a period of nearly a year she wrote more than fifty thousand words which she handed over to her spiritual adviser, Bishop Eric Eades of the Holy Celtic Church, to read and interpret.

On May 6th as the stigmata on her left hand began to emerge Heather had a vision of Jesus being baptized and drew a picture of what she saw. Four days later she had a vision of Christ on the cross, which she also drew, and she was told at that stage that in sixty-three days' time she would witness a transfiguration that would take her from her old life to a new beginning. Heather also believed at that stage that her marks should be kept a secret to herself and her spiritual counsellor until she was ready to show her doctor and others in the Church. It was nearly a year before the marks became public knowledge. Her doctor, who had known Heather for over twenty years, was shown the marks in June and he has confirmed in writing that he was satisfied they were spontaneous lesions for which he could offer no medical explanation.

Her writings cover a wide range of mystical subjects. They are recorded with her left hand, even though she is normally right-handed. The handwriting is clear, but the style can vary distinctly from paragraph to paragraph. Much of her writing is done at night when she spends long periods in prayer and meditation.

These examples of her writings will give some flavour of the message she has felt compelled to convey. In June she wrote at one o'clock one morning:

Oh to be more like Jesus Christ! In view of all that He has done for us, this should be the testimony of everyone who knows Him as saviour. May He be the object of our love, the joy of our lives, and the one we aspire to be like. May He be our whole purpose for living.

Two days later at 2.25 a.m. Heather wrote:

Rudeness is putting people down in order to try to hold ourselves up, but love is never rude because love is the power that moves towards people for their good alone.

In October this was a message she received:

Those days are troubled ones. Predictions by a variety of brilliant men will strike fear into your heart, but together be thankful for the fact that you are being made aware of the insecurity, and thank your Father for the security of insecurity. Your action must be to run to your Father, to more solid ground, the most dependable safe place available in the universe. All other ground is sinking sand.

And a month later at midnight Heather wrote:

Once we have learnt the discipline of a controlled tongue, help us, Lord, to put our words to good use . . . May we meditate on the blessings we have received and may our hearts be full of joy as our faith grows ever deeper, grounded on Jesus, our rock and our redeemer.

Heather's prophecy that she was to receive a transfiguration was fulfilled in an unexpected way. Heather's son Lindsey was convinced that his mother was going to die, but she felt that the transfiguration prophecy had another meaning. When the sixty-three days were up, Heather believes the period of the prophecy began, culminating on a day in September. What seems to have happened is that during that period when the prophecy was being fulfilled, Heather's health deteriorated to a point when again her friends expected her not to live. However on the night when she was at her lowest and in greatest pain from her medical condition, taking prescribed morphine on a regular basis, she had a vision and experience she now interprets as the climax of the prophecy. She had been at a service at the small chapel in Bishop Eades' house and was taken back to her own home. Although she remembers very little of that evening, what she does recall clearly is the feeling she had, as in a dream or vision, of moving down a small beach of sand towards two men knee-deep in water. One held his hand out to her.

I knew I had to walk to him and yet I was compelled to turn round. So I turned and there were hundreds of people just all looking at me. There was eye contact with them all and it was wonderful.

I was actually drawn to this one man in the water, who had his hands turned out to me, but it was like walking in warm oil rather than water because it embraced me, it took over the whole of me. I took hold of this man's hands and I remember being lowered into what felt like the warm oil and then being in a room with one man accompanied by ten others. I was dripping wet. Each of the ten men came towards me and embraced me. I wondered what was happening. I looked round the room and it was as if there were no corners, it wasn't a very big room and the roof was low although the men were quite tall, there was something like straw on the floor. I'd never seen anything like it, but I had this feeling that I belonged there. After each man had come and hugged me I saw another man sitting down and putting his hand out to me, I moved towards him and took hold of his hand, I knew he was our Lord. I closed my eyes while we were holding hands and I was on the cross with Christ, but there was no pain. I was looking into His face and it was as if we were one, there was this wonderful feeling of compassion and wholeness. Then the next minute I was sitting in my chair at home absolutely wet through, it was nine minutes past three in the morning.

I looked down and my hands were bleeding.

The next day, Bishop Eric and Heather's doctor both saw that she had renewed vigour and health. 'My doctor couldn't believe it, he hugged me and we cried.' Despite her doctor's warnings, Heather decided not to take morphine any more, she said she did not need it because she was so convinced she was healed.

Heather like many stigmatics before her has had a difficult life. As a child she was sent to a children's home from which on many occasions she attempted to escape. Her parents were divorced and she recalls being regarded as a difficult and problem child. She remembers that at the age of fourteen she began to pray. It was at the time that her parents were being divorced. She married at the age of twenty but her husband Ray died after twelve years after a short illness and Heather was left with the responsibilities of being a single mother.

From the age of fourteen onwards I have prayed every night without a miss, even in hospital after all the surgery. I feel humble and privileged to have a relationship with God. I strongly believe that miracles are not a thing of the past. They still do happen. The marks on my hands and feet impel me to spread the message that people should ask Jesus to come into their lives and that they should ask him to forgive their sins. Salvation and eternal life will mean a time when there will be no more pain. This is the message I have been given in my writings. The marks are the physical sign that something amazing has happened although there are many who still can't believe what they see. Still doubt that I have been healed. I have been warned that I will be ridiculed. But I am growing spiritually.

On Good Friday 1993 a service was held in the chapel at Bishop Eades' house attended by a small group of members of the Holy Celtic Church congregation in Lincoln. Bishop Eades at that stage was himself very ill and indeed was to die shortly afterwards from a long illness. Towards the end of a simple service in which the suffering of Christ was recalled, Heather appeared to be distressed. There were tears in her eyes, she looked to be in pain and needed to sit. Immediately after the service she explained that at that very moment she had felt a pain in her side and a feeling of deep involvement with the suffering of Jesus on the cross. She and others present examined the wound on her side and it was seen to have been bleeding. The blood had dried and the bleeding must have taken place some time before her moment of distress in the service but after the examination of her side which had taken place three hours earlier that day.

Two days later, Easter Day, Heather had a mark of a cross on her forehead, the second time this had happened to her. It remained visible to her and others for a number of days.

Television pictures of her experience on Good Friday were shown on network television in Britain a week later and created considerable interest. Heather received letters from people around the country wanting her to pray for them and Heather felt that the purpose behind what she saw as the gift of the stigmata was that, not only would it be a witness to the miraculous, but that she had also received a gift of healing. When Bishop Eades died Heather converted a room in her small terraced house into a chapel for his congregation and held healing services there. It was a summer of intense activity for her, but during that time her health deteriorated. She lost weight which she could ill afford to lose and had a spell in hospital having collapsed at home. By July and August she was again in intense pain and taking morphine but she was on what she describes as a 'spiritual high'. One curious event which took place, which could not have been replicated by the earlier stigmatics in the age before photography, was that a vision of an arc of light which Heather describes seeing in the chapel at her home, was captured by a camera. Heather described the arc of light as being the presence of the Holy Spirit and seeing it was not a new experience to her. However she knew that others could not see it. Nevertheless when the light appeared to her in the chapel she asked the widow of Bishop Eades to come to the chapel with her and to bring her camera. Betty Eades saw nothing extraordinary but took a photograph of the altar and chapel decorations. When this picture was developed an arc of light appeared on the exposed film which, says Heather, corresponded to the light of the Holy Spirit she could see. The light on the photograph will no doubt be dismissed by sceptics as the product of camera or photographer error. A later picture which Heather believes shows the light of the Holy Spirit in the room was returned to her with the advice from the developers that the picture had been overexposed. Heather is convinced however that no mundane explanation is satisfactory.

Similarly with the healings which Heather believes have taken place. Sceptics will argue, as they have done on other occasions, that people who report experiences of miraculous recoveries may only be reporting short-term remissions. Nevertheless Heather is convinced some amazing recoveries have taken place as a result of the ministry which has developed following her stigmatization.

Another modern case of stigmata which has been well documented and which has also within it a number of elements associated with the stigmatics of old is that of Ethel Chapman. She was nearly fifty-three when she joined the select group of people who have received the marks of Christ.

She had been ill for many years with multiple sclerosis, a condition which had cut short her career as a dancer and entertainer. Easter 1974 saw Ethel in hospital. She was in almost constant pain and her limbs were subject to uncontrollable spasms and her legs had to be weighted down by the hospital traction equipment to prevent them jerking up violently knocking her knees against her chin. She was very ill, not only from her chronic condition but from septicaemia caused through a bedsore. She was not at that stage a religious person, but had formed a friendship with a Christian woman who had visited her in the ward and had given her an illustrated Bible.

Before going to sleep on the night of the Saturday before Easter Ethel had been looking at the Bible and had seen in it a picture of the crucifixion. Ethel wanted to find a faith and make some sense of her illness and recalls her prayer that night, 'Oh Lord, show me in some way if you're there.'

For many years Ethel had been quite cynical about the Church, particularly as her physical condition declined. Yet on that night before Easter she was not in the mood for cynicism. She did not expect to live long and the prayer was a despairing cry of a broken woman.

That night Ethel Chapman had a dream.

In the early hours of the morning, I felt myself being drawn onto the cross. I felt the pain of the nails through my hands and through my feet. I could see the crowds all jeering and shouting. It was in a foreign language so I don't know what they were saying. I felt in myself all the pain and all the agony the Lord himself went through. I myself was in the Lord's body.

In a later account of her vision she wrote that that night she had been restless and could not sleep.

Suddenly I had the weird sensation of being lifted off the bed and floating through the crowds. I felt myself being pulled onto the cross. I didn't know what was happening. I had the agonizing sensation of metal tearing into flesh as the first nail was driven into the palm of my hand. Then I felt my wrists being bound and the cross being pushed up into the sky. The pain in my hands was unbearable. At that moment I knew the excruciating pain Christ suffered. I felt very close to God.

Early on Easter morning when the nurses came to wash her, they noticed Ethel's hands were bleeding. For the next six years, until her death in 1980 at the age of fifty-nine, Ethel carried the stigmata. She relived the experience of her vision each year around Easter. For the first two years it was on Easter Sunday, then it was Easter Monday and after that Good Friday. The vision never changed. Later as she relived her crucifixion she was fully conscious, although afterwards she went into a deep sleep. She came to believe that it was her duty to go through with the pain.

From the start her vision and wounds were taken seriously by the hospital staff and Ethel recalled that the doctor who first examined her was a devout Roman Catholic who recognized a prima facie case of stigmata and alerted the hospital chaplaincy.

Apart from Easter, Ethel's wounds bled and reopened from time to time at moments of stress or, she believed, to warn her of events. To her they were a form of premonition, usually of a death. She would feel a jab or pinprick in her hands and soon the wounds would open.

The marks on her hands were just off-centre and her feet were similarly marked. She also had other forms of bruising and what appeared to be a rope mark on her wrist. Around her forehead she had a few dotted pinpricks which, it was suggested to her, could have corresponded to the marks of a crown of thorns. She described a feeling in her visions which could have tallied with wearing such a crown; 'I felt a heaviness and soreness'.

In addition to her visions of crucifixion, Ethel Chapman had other visions. Once she felt she was walking on the water with Christ and for a time afterwards her multiple

sclerosis went into a period of remission which enabled
her to walk unaided. Also in a similar state she felt herself
walking up the steps of the temple and again, this time
during a bout of muscle spasm, she felt a hand on her
shoulder which she felt was the hand of Christ. She heard
a voice saying, 'my child, this is the end of your pain and
suffering', and her pain vanished.

Ethel also described a vision of Heaven in which she
was walking through a garden and was held close to Christ.
She could smell a sweet perfume in the air. She would
describe too how when her hands bled she was aware of
a fragrance of roses.

> When I see Heaven, the Lord is real but the other
> figures are very shadowy. I always know what He
> is saying to me. I hear the words: although He is
> speaking a foreign language, I can understand. I've
> often thought that when I have visited Heaven it's
> as a spirit. I've left my body back on earth. I don't
> doubt that I have seen Heaven. It's a beautiful place.
> Purple is the prevalent colour and lilac. There are
> bright lights and chandeliers. Christ usually has a
> white robe on. I always see His hands and His feet.
> I see Jesus as He is.

More than just giving her a picture of Heaven and of Jesus,
Ethel's visions gave her a feeling of contentment and
tranquillity. She also described feelings of lightness, as if
being lifted off her bed.

Although her marks were visible and she showed them
to people she trusted, no-one ever saw her levitate and her

reports of fragrances were subjective and uncorroborated. Yet they tally with similar descriptions of events and sensations experienced in earlier centuries.

She did not become the centre of a Christian subcult in the way that other stigmatists have done, but her experience could not be kept to a small circle of people and both local and national newspapers ran articles telling her story. People wrote to her asking for her prayers and Ethel believed that through her was channelled a healing power. Sometimes those who wrote to her sent a handkerchief or piece of cloth asking that she place them on her wounds when they bled. Ethel believed that her stigmata were signs that her life's suffering had not been in vain, and that they were also a sign that she had work to do to help others through the power of healing. Her latter years were spent at a Leonard Cheshire home and Ethel spent much time in her room with her own thoughts, praying for others but having less and less contact with other people.

When Ethel was born at Whitsun in 1921 her grandmother declared that Ethel had been born 'a child of God'. For many years Ethel did not know what that meant but at the end of her life believed that it was a reference to the stigmata. Her father died from his First World War wounds when Ethel was young and her memories of him were only those of him when ill and disabled. She followed a family tradition and became an entertainer, billed as Ethel Chiverton, the comedy girl. She appeared in a double act with her brother as well as sharing the bill with entertainers ranging from a seventeen-year-old Hughie Green to the world-famous American bandleader Glen Miller. Her career came to an end when her face became paralysed and she began to stumble on stage. It was the onset of multiple sclerosis and Ethel was bitter and angry. From then on her life was a rough one. She married, but discovered after two years that her husband was a bigamist. She ran a small shop but the work became increasingly difficult as the illness progressed. Her daughter helped out and as Ethel became increasingly immobile she turned her general store into a self-service shop. Eventually however the pain and the disability became too much. It was as a patient at the Birkenhead General Hospital that Ethel, in considerable pain and believing her life to be at an end, had the profound religious experience which gave a purpose to her final years.

Her marks were taken seriously by the Anglican Bishop of Liverpool, David Sheppard, who met Ethel and found her to be a person of simple but profound faith. He delegated a local parish priest, Rev. David Lockyer, to act as her mentor. Ethel was also examined by, amongst others, a geriatrician Dr Colin Powell who commented that she was a 'totally integrated personality, exhibiting no signs of emotion. She was one of the most complete and peaceful people I have ever met.' He also confirmed impressions made by other medical people that there was no suggestion that her marks were produced by 'the obsessive scratching of the skin which can be a symptom of certain types of psychological disorder'.

In her last years Ethel's disability prevented her from reaching her feet with her hands, but nevertheless the feet remained marked by the wounds. And although the first marks could have been self-produced, although not intentionally to deceive, during her initial vivid dream, by clenching her fists and digging a fingernail into her flesh, this explanation is unlikely. For the marks continued to reappear often under observation and as a multiple sclerosis patient Ethel would not have had the physical strength to make the marks.

Ethel found comfort in the thought that the stigmata were a sign that she was not alone in her suffering and that she was united with Christ through her pain. When she died in July 1980 the marks remained on her body.

Ethel was one of those stigmatists about whom it was said that she had extraordinary gifts of insight. In this respect she was similar to the best known stigmatist of the twentieth century, Padre Pio, who was said to be able to see into people's hearts and know what was going on many miles away from where he lived. In Ethel's case she believed she had a gift of clairvoyance and could foresee the deaths of people close to her.

There was an unexpected death in the home where I lived. My hands bled very heavily that night. The gentleman went into hospital and nobody had any idea he was so poorly, in fact the staff here didn't realize that it was dehydration and he passed away. It was a shock to everyone, even the doctors.

As my hands were bleeding I did not know who my hands were bleeding for. I don't always know. But if there's someone ill in the home I do know. I feel a special closeness to them.

Ethel also spoke of people coming to her room at night at the time of their death. She talked of hugging them close and being at one with them even though in reality the people in question were in another place and could not possibly travel except in spirit or her imagination.

I hear the voices of people who are about to die. And I can sometimes see them, they come to my room.

And Ethel described in an interview she gave shortly before her death a particular instance.

Once I turned around and saw a person sitting in my chair. I was in bed at the time. It should have been impossible because she was in hospital. But in my mind she was there sitting in the chair. In my imagination she was there in my room.

She thanked me for saying prayers for her. She said, 'I'm going to die, but I'm not going to die in pain.' I have never put my hand out to reach anyone who has come to my room. They're too far away, in the doorway. My bed is the other side of the room and they all seem to sit in the doorway. They're always in their wheelchairs even though they may not have been out of their sickbed for a long time. When they come to me, they're in a wheelchair.

I feel so much love for them, I just want to give them a hug, but I can't, much as I would like to. I can't get to them. But I've no doubt that they're there. And they're waiting for me.

Ethel was reluctant to commit to tape her recollections of people feeling close to her in bed when they were about to die, but she did describe this weird experience.

> I knew when Pope John Paul was going to die. It was a funny sensation. I felt someone coming to grip hold of me tight. I thought it was somebody real who had got into bed with me. And the person said, 'It's all right, it's only Paul' and I couldn't connect who Paul was. And he kept talking about popes and then he said, 'I won't be here tomorrow, I won't be here tomorrow, I won't be here tomorrow', the voice just fading away.
>
> I told the staff what had happened and they told me the next morning that the Pope had died. I had that feeling too of being held before my mother died.

She told few people about these feelings. Of the many strange things that had happened to her, this was the one about which she felt most uneasy. So, for what reason did she get these sensations? She was not able to go and see the people who visited her in ghostly form and reassure them. There was little point in telling the residents and the staff about her premonitions too often. It alarmed some people and some of her premonitions even caused herself disquiet.

Her spiritual adviser David Lockyer said of Ethel that she was an example of someone not wishing to have had the stigmata.

> In her condition she had enough to contend with in her struggle for life.

When asked how the marks were produced he turned the question on its head:

> We can look at possibilities, hysteria of an egotist, the welling up of the unconscious, divine intervention at a time of ecstatic experience. Does it matter where the explanation lies? . . . There seems no good reason why Padre Pio should have been given the stigmata and Saint Augustine not: Or why Ethel Chapman should have received the marks and not Mother Teresa.

In the case of Jane Hunt she also received the marks quite unexpectedly but in very different circumstances. She was twenty-eight years old at the time and the marks remained with her for two years. She is a wife and mother and lives in an ordinary house in the small Derbyshire community of Codnor. At the time of her stigmatization her husband was working as a bus driver and they had one daughter. Jane describes herself as 'nothing special, just an ordinary woman'. Like Ethel she is an Anglican and was given a conventional religious upbringing attending Sunday school and religious education classes at school. She is a member of the congregation at her local Church of England parish church but not a regular attender. Like Ethel she has had a history of bad health. Jane suffered a period of deafness during childhood, experienced two miscarriages as an adult and most recently has been operated on for cancer.

On the evening of 24 July 1985 she reports having seen the face of Jesus on her pillow as she went to bed and that night, she says, she had a vision of a brilliant white figure standing by her bed.

> It was so brilliant I couldn't make out any face, it was just like a light shining. The figure stood at the side of the bed and I was quite content. I wasn't frightened and he slowly disappeared.

The next morning, which was the feast of the patron saint of her local church, St James, as Jane prepared breakfast, her hands seemed to itch and burn. At 10 a.m., as she left the house to go shopping, she experienced a sudden and tremendous pain in her hands as if needles were being driven through them. Blood began to flow from the centre of the palms.

> It just started seeping through the skin. There were no holes or anything to speak of.

She remembers being very frightened.

> I just got through the gate and came running back as they started to bleed. My husband sat me on a chair and I showed him what had happened. We weren't sure whether we should tell anybody but I thought that I must tell the parish priest.

She told the priest, Rev. Norman Hill, what had happened and, she recalls 'he was full of smiles and very happy'. He identified the marks as stigmata and took her experience seriously. The appearance of the marks also followed shortly after the time in her life when Jane first felt able to forgive her father for what she describes as 'things which happened in the past' (a reference to abuse).

Around Easter and on a number of Sundays the wounds were particularly sensitive and in a twenty-four-hour period Jane estimated she could lose up to a pint of blood. When active the centres of her hands appeared to blister and then burst. Deep fissuring was observed but her hands were not pierced. In addition to the marks on her hands, Jane twice reported seeing small marks on her feet and felt a severe pain in her right side. Jane did not show the marks to her doctor, although there was one occasion when she needed to attend a hospital casualty department where the wounds were noticed by a nursing sister, but they aroused no special curiosity.

> She saw the stigmata marks and put her finger on them and asked what they were and when I said stigmata she looked at me quite blankly. Whether she knew what I meant or whether she was thinking, this woman is crazy, I don't know but she just carried on doing what she was doing and that was the end of that.

The first 'mystical' experience Jane recalls was an 'out-of-body' sensation. She was at the time in hospital and her heart stopped beating during a medical crisis at the time of the birth of her daughter. Later she described seeing her own body being worked on by medical staff and also being aware of a door through which, she believed, she could choose to go. She describes feeling very close to God,

71

who, according to her description, chose to send her back. She was receiving a number of medical drugs at the time.

Over the next four years she describes other experiences which, she says, enabled her to relate to God very easily, after which she first began to experience burning and itching feelings in the hands.

Shortly after her hands began to bleed Jane was at prayer when, she says, she heard the voice of Jesus reassuring her that he would never leave her. Jane, in trying to describe her experience, has talked of sometimes feeling as if she were inside Christ. She finds it hard to describe the sensation other than to say 'I just feel safe, nobody can hurt me, I am content, I am at peace within.'

I think all Christians would like to take the burden of His pain. I am sure none of us would have wanted Him to suffer and I wonder had I been there at His crucifixion would I have said sacrifice me not Christ? But it is God's will that He was crucified and who are we to tell God what to do? I am however now taking on His pain. I don't think I am taking the pain that He really suffered. I can cope with my pain, but Christ suffered more than I will ever know.

When a child, from the age of five, Jane had lived in a house opposite a chapel in the village of Ripley in Derbyshire. From her bedroom she could see a stained-glass window showing a nativity scene. This image set her imagination going.

I used to go to bed at night and I could see the holy family living there at the church. I had a perfect picture in my mind of what they were doing, I would watch Mary rocking the baby in the crib, I would see all the cattle, the goats, the donkeys, it was very real to me and very beautiful.

She has never forgotten the window and some of the images contained in it, and which she created in her imagination from it, appear to have formed the basis of the visions she was to see as an adult.

In describing one of these adult visions she tells of the feeling of being transported to Bethlehem and being allowed to hold the Christ child. In another vision she saw Mary in her own house. Her husband, who was in the room at the time, did not see the vision. Jane talks too of visiting Christ and feeling his arms around her and 'sinking into His body'. She was also disturbed, she says, by experiencing a vision of the devil who tried to undermine her faith. She has also detected an unexplained sweet smell of roses in her house, a scent which her mother and husband also noticed. On one occasion, during what she believes were visits by or experiences of Jesus, she saw another person who was unknown to her. She later recognized the man from a photograph shown to her by a friend. He was her friend's father who had died that night. At the same time she had another curious precognition that a friend's pet tortoise had also died.

As an adult her visions are very real to her. Sometimes when she had seen Mary in her own house Jane describes herself as being awake and the figure of Mary being substantial. 'I can be doing things around the house when I see her standing there.' On other occasions Jane's visions come to her when she is deep in prayer. 'I feel I am leaving my body behind and I go to wherever Jesus calls me.'

Jane does not doubt that her stigmata was a spiritual gift. Initially she was very reluctant to show her marks to anyone other than her family and priest. She wore gloves when in public. Later she came to believe that she had a healing ministry. She was encouraged in this by Father Hill after Jane was able to relieve him of some of the pain of abscesses on his leg. For a while she took part in healing services in the local church. She would wear a white dress and headscarf and as word spread in the community these healing services became well attended. During these services, she laid her hands on people who came forward. Cures have been reported, but no independent verification is available.

> People don't come to me, they come to God. I pray that the Lord will use me as his instrument to take away all the bad. Because I am not worthy to do this, he empties me of myself, we swap roles and Christ fills me. I feel his spirit come through me and then I turn to the people and heal them. I am not totally aware of what I am doing because Christ moves me. I feel like a light, electricity, a power coming through and the people say they get a warm feeling. It is very emotional.

There is no way of proving that Jane Hunt's marks were not self-inflicted. She was physically capable of causing them and had the opportunity. Her recollection of the chronology of events surrounding the appearance of her marks has not been consistent. But she kept no record of events at the time and it could be suggested that if she was involved in fraud she would have taken the trouble to develop a consistent story. Given that she had only received a basic education, it would also seem very unlikely that she would have known about the other mystical phenomena commonly associated with stigmata, which she herself reported as having experienced. She has appeared to all who have met her to be a plausible witness and to be telling the truth as she has experienced it. Also given her initial reluctance to show off her marks, it could be said that she had no desire to get them and no motive for deliberately creating them.

Jane Hunt's stigmata lasted until 1987 and faded following a hysterectomy. Her experience, not unexpectedly, made a profound impact on her, but she continues to refer to herself, and in no sense of false modesty, as 'a very ordinary person. I'm just Jane'.

The case of George H is somewhat different although his marks appeared at about the same time as those of Jane. He lives in a public housing flat on an estate on the outskirts of Glasgow. He is unemployed and a Roman Catholic in his forties. He shares his home with his partner but says that he lives a celibate life. He is also a lay Franciscan. His marks first appeared shortly before Lent in 1986.

He was not especially observant as a member of his church, but was, at the time, reading about and contemplating the nature of the Turin Shroud and had a special interest in St Francis of Assisi. He woke one morning to find the backs of his hands bleeding.

When I first noticed it I thought my nose was bleeding and I put my hand up to it. But then I realized the blood wasn't coming from my nose and I noticed the marks on my hands.

The marks on the top of his feet appeared later but they did not bleed immediately.

When I walk across the carpet in my bare feet I feel as though I'm standing on a pebble.

Subsequently his hands have bled regularly. Occasionally small marks appear in his palms. The upper sides of his feet also bleed and the soles of his feet, he reports, are painful to walk on. He has also received marks, as of scourging, on his back, a wound in his right side, and bruising on one shoulder, as if he has been carrying a heavy object or as if his shoulder has been dislocated or punched. He says that he experiences severe pain most days. By 1992 George was experiencing something else associated with stigmatists of the past, he was unable to eat and retain any solid food. He had become very thin and had a tube inserted through his nose through which liquid food could be passed to his stomach. His doctor could find no organic cause for this inability to eat solid food and when referred to a psychiatrist for assessment, the psychiatrist reported he could find no reason to believe that George was suffering from any psychiatric illness.

He kept his hands covered by mittens and even though his marks went for periods of time without bleeding, a discoloured area of skin was always visible and he was seldom free from pain. Indeed his pain was often worse when the marks were quiet. His wounds were beginning to follow an anticipated cycle of activity with new bleeding occurring in Lent leading up to Holy Week.

Much of his day and night are spent in prayer asking God for help in understanding what has happened to him. He says that God replies to his prayers, 'although not that I hear a voice'. He is also concerned that people he knows snub him and reject him when they learn about the stigmata. He says that he would rather be left alone to cope with it. When George showed the marks to his parish priest, the priest 'went into a state of shock', then told him to see his doctor. George reports no further help from the local church. The bishop however took a greater interest and told George that what had happened was a miracle and that he should use it for the healing ministry. He finds that people do come to him for healing, but is wary, as many of those who come, he feels, just want him to touch them for superstitious reasons.

George claims that remarks are made about him as he passes in the street and he is nervous when he goes out into the community.

> Hoping no-one will come up behind me with their baby asking me to touch them or something like that. It happened once and just because I said no to the woman she gave me a mouthful so I went home and left her.

George no longer attends Mass regularly as this normally results in him disrupting the service. He experiences what can perhaps be described as a religious ecstasy when taking communion. He finds he loses sense of time and place, and to outward appearances would seem to be under the influence of a drug. His few attendances at church are away from his local area where the priest is more accepting of his condition.

George reports having visions of Jesus twice, when he felt as if he had entered another world. On one of those occasions Jesus was accompanied by Mary who told George that 'her son was unhappy with the way he, George, was being treated'. When the experience was repeated a third time, George describes a feeling of unease and believes he was confronted by the devil. The devil threatened him with harm and George believes the threat was carried out when the front door of his house was set alight and a dead cat was exhumed from his garden. A particularly alarming incident occurred when he heard a voice speaking to him and mocking him from a tape of music which he had put on his cassette player. George was convinced the voice was not pre-recorded as it addressed him by name and reacted to his responses. He no longer has the tape, having given it to a priest and it is not available to be tested.

The first time I saw Jesus I felt good. Everything around me seemed to disappear, there was no noise, I couldn't hear the kids on the street or any cars passing. I wasn't aware of any sounds in the house, the cat jumping about or anything like that. The second time I was also in that state when I saw Jesus and the Virgin Mary. It was then she said that He did not like the way I was being treated. That was it, everything disappeared again.

The third time I got the image again and it was an exact replica of the Jesus figure I had seen but I sensed there was something wrong. There was a coldness in the air and I was told that I did not have to take communion. I came out with the words 'you're not Jesus'. Most people would say, grab holy water and do this or that, but when you're in that state you're not aware of what you're doing, it's impossible to move. So all I could say, the conversation was coming from the mind, was 'you're not Jesus'. As I said this the figure pointed his finger at me and threatened to get me. I was terrified, I knew my feelings were correct and that this was the devil.

George describes himself as 'nothing special' and not 'particularly good or even-tempered'. God, he says, could have picked someone better than him for the marks. He says he does not feel happy having the marks, except during prayer. Then, he says, he feels close to Christ, who understands the sense of rejection George feels, as He Himself also experienced it when on earth. George insists he does not want to become famous. 'I am not a circus piece', are his words.

It is physically possible that George produced the marks himself. However there is no evidence that this is so, indeed if he had intended to produce some form of pious fraud, it is unlikely that he would have chosen to produce wounds in his hands which are not consistent with the reports of wounds in the hands of previous stigmatists, in that the recurring wounds appear on the upper side only. His doctor, who has examined him, also has no reason to suspect self-infliction of wounds.

George says that it is only when he is at prayer that he feels at ease about his stigmata.

Most of the time otherwise I am accompanied by pain. People imagine that I must be walking in a seventh heaven, but it's not like that. The good moments are very few and far between and very precious.

Although they share their Catholicism and the same Christian tradition the worlds of George in working-class Glasgow and that of Father Jim Bruse in Lake Ridge just outside Washington D.C. could not be a greater contrast.

Father Bruse is an assistant priest at a thriving suburban church dedicated to Saint Elizabeth Ann Seton. The day after Christmas in 1991 he too became a stigmatic, but in a very public way. His experience was widely reported in the press, attracted considerable attention from television stations and the numbers of people attending the church rose dramatically. His experience coincided with another curious phenomenon which members of the congregation had claimed to witness, statues of the Virgin Mary appearing to weep tears.

In March 1992 the *Washington Post* described the events in this way.

'Uh, see that one's crying now,' he says. 'The one on the bookcase.'

'Okay, yeah, Father Jimbo, let's just get on with the interview.'

'That one over there,' he says quietly, pointing to a foot-high statue of the Blessed Mother.

'It's an optical trick. They've rigged the lighting in here.'

'No, go ahead, go over and look at it,' he says with a kind of small weariness. 'You can pick it up. Go ahead, taste it with your finger. Turn it around, look under it,' he says.

There are four people in this room. The door is closed. There are at least half a dozen statues of Mary in here and also color enlargements on the walls of zoo animals, the kind weekend photo buffs make. The four people present are a priest and three journalists. The print reporter is the first to put his pencil down and approach the bookcase. It's about seven feet away.

Then a reporter from Channel 5. And then her T-shirted cameraman. There's something entirely new in his demeanor.

The statue, which has a halo and seems to be made of plaster, is on a fake wood bookcase. There are no visible wires. No battery-operated tear ducts like a religious Chatty Cathy with a hole in her back where you put in the size C's. This statue seems actually to be producing water. The water, from what the naked eye can tell, is forming at the corner of the right eye. But the eye is very small and so it is hard to know for sure.

The *Washington Post* reporter is standing maybe

four inches from the Blessed Mother's nose. There's gotta be a trick here. It's as if the water is just appearing right out of the plaster and then rolling downward.

A bead forms under the alabaster pink chin. It swells. BLOP, it falls. There are four tiny puddles of water at the statue's base now. Proof positive you can be seeing something and still not believe you're seeing it.

Father Bruse tells of how at the previous Christmas there had been a series of statues that had been weeping and changing colour.

I then noticed that it was after I had touched statues that this began. And then my wrist started bleeding. I didn't know what it was. And when I went out to the store my feet starting hurting real bad. When I got home they were bleeding and a little later my right side started bleeding too. I couldn't figure out what it was. I discussed it with the Bishop and he sent me to a doctor to check it out. I wanted to know if it was a skin disease or something. When I was with the doctor the marks were bleeding at the time, the blood was like a light red color blood, I remember sitting there and the blood was draining to the side. I could actually hold my hand down but the blood wouldn't go down, it would go off to the side defying gravity. And I could smell roses from it. This was all written down in a report and sent to the Bishop. And then through January, February,

March and April the bleeding was really heavy. By June it had quietened down. At other times I had what I call the inner stigmata when I had pain. The wrists would be very painful and then the feet and the side. It would happen sometimes at night or when I was driving the car all of a sudden. Yet along with the pain came these sensations, these beautiful sensations.

And at that time Father Bruse says the sensation is accompanied by a serene sound.

It's almost like singing, it's a sound of that nature. It sounds like voices, but I can't be sure. The mind can't capture it all. But the biggest thing that happens with all this is color. It's like feeling and touching color, and the colors come up into a fan shape, and come into me, I can feel that happening at times. I can feel the color, touch it and it's beautiful and that's when I hear the sound. I guess it's singing, I just cannot put my finger on what it is. But it's very beautiful, it's very peaceful, very serene.

Father Bruse also describes a time when at his desk he had the feeling that he could see Calvary.

I could see the hill, I could see the crosses and the pain was really intense that time. I even drew a picture of it. There was one of the secretaries there and she could see how bad the pain was, and I kept

telling her I was seeing something. And I sat there
and drew it, a picture of the hill of Calvary with the
crosses. But it was only the one time that happened.

Father Jim Bruse was ordained in 1979. He is now thirty-
seven and in every other way a typical parish priest. In
appearance he's a very unlikely mystic with his bushy
moustache and high American leather boots and large ring
on his hand. Prior to the extraordinary events of 1991–2
Father Bruse says that he had, like many priests, fallen into
a routine.

> Sometimes even Mass was becoming a routine and
> that's how I was beginning to feel. But all these
> events just smashed through that, it was like the
> supernatural breaking into reality, it was dramatic.

The supernatural element of the breakthrough astounded
both Jim Bruse and his congregation. Things began to
happen in their church which would have been more
familiar to a medieval community than one based in the
twentieth-century United States.

> The wildest thing that happened concerned a small
> statue of Our Lady of Fatima. I blessed it one day
> during confession and the color started moving on
> it. There was color, a tint already on the statue but
> the color started to move and we brought the statue
> up to the front of the church and two hundred
> people who were downstairs playing bingo, came up
> and they could see it for themselves. That was two

hundred people who witnessed it and it was dramatic. For about fifty minutes it was adding colors and subtracting colors. The colors were moving and rotating on the statue. There was, I'm quite sure, no light shining on the statue. We had the regular church lights on but these colors in the statue were blue, green, pink, orange, yellow and kept rotating around. The light in the church didn't have that effect.

I explain it all as Christ saying that He wants His people to come back. He is saying that Mary is there to intercede. It has been her image and her statues that have been changing color and weeping. I think she plays a part in it. I definitely feel it's from Christ, there's no doubt about it. I just wish I knew why I had a part to play in it all. Everything was just going along normally, when suddenly, bam, it all happened.

And things are not just happening here. In New Jersey there's a statue changing color and in Ohio there's an icon crying and in Arizona they're saying that they're having apparitions and in Texas too statues are crying and in Florida and in Kentucky strange things are happening.

I feel sorry for the priests in the places where these sorts of things happen. They'll get hit by a deluge of interest.

Father Bruse said speaking in August 1992.

We're having that just now. Waves of people and on some days, ordinary weekdays, there are four hundred people for Mass, where normally eight might have shown up before all this happened. These are visitors coming from all over the world. They fly in either to see the statue or just to get a blessing and they're happy with that. It's amazing. It blows your mind when you see it. It's all so beautiful, it's done wonders. Some people say that it's all from Satan, and say that I am the devil, and I say how can this be when so many people are being converted, coming back to Christ through these events. There are people being healed physically and spiritually. What I see is all positive.

The priest in charge of the parish, Father Daniel Hamilton, is a man of fifty, with twenty years experience as a priest behind him. Until his colleague's experience, his faith had never depended on signs and wonders.

But I have now seen Jim Bruse. I know what I see and I'm not given to visions. I have seen his wrists bleed, once the blood was all over the carpet in the rectory.

Father Hamilton has also seen the activated statues, and has even seen one of them bleeding.

I doubted it all at the beginning. Are you crazy? Holy smoke! Guy who works for me . . . walks into my office, goes on about the whole thing. That he's got statues that are crying and so forth, that he has this funny bleeding. And I am sitting here, right at this same desk, looking at him, listening to him, and I'm saying to myself as he's talking and I'm listening to all this crap, 'hey, buddy, if you think what you're telling me is true, I'm not going to have you as my assistant much longer. You're whacko.' And then, like I say, I saw some of this stuff he'd been talking about. It's true. That's all I can tell you. It's true.

And many of the curious events have been witnessed by other members of the congregation.

Jim Bruse is not the only modern case of stigmata on the American side of the Atlantic.

In 1972 a ten-year-old black girl, Cloretta Robinson, living in California, was found to have bleeding from the palm of her left hand which occurred from two to six times daily. The bleeding began when she was in her classroom at school. She experienced no pain with it and gave no sign of any emotional change at the time. At the time she was in excellent health and her family had no history of prolonged bleeding, easy bruising or psychiatric disorder. Cloretta lived with her forty-six-year-old mother who was a dental technician, her stepfather, her older sister and her four children and a brother. By all accounts the home although crowded and modest was a happy place and the family were active attenders at a Baptist church near their home.

At the first medical examination by Dr Laretta Early, a pediatric physician from the West Oakland Health Center, dried blood was found on her left palm, bleeding having occurred some ten minutes earlier. When the blood was washed away there were no lesions visible. Even when the bleeding sites were examined under a magnifying glass all that was seen was normal skin. Medical reports described her as 'a pleasant, neatly and attractively groomed, prepubescent black girl, cheerful and friendly . . . she was alert, well-orientated . . . and her school work was low/average'. After her first medical examination her left hand was bound and she returned to school and within three hours, while in the classroom, her right palm began to bleed. On the sixth day of her experience there was bleeding from her left foot, a day later the right foot, a day after that there was bleeding from her right side and on the fourteenth day from the middle of her forehead. This was seven days before Easter Sunday.

Writing in the *Archive of General Psychiatry* of February 1974, Dr J. E. Lifschutz and Dr L. F. Early, wrote

for a total of nineteen days various persons and the patient reported bleeding from these sites, usually one to five times daily, but with the frequency decreasing to once every two days. She bled from the hands more frequently than from the other sites. Numerous instances of blood appearing on all sites were observed by her schoolteachers, the school nurse, her physician and other hospital staff.

Several accounts were reported of skin which appeared to have no marks or lesions oozing blood over a one- to four-minute time span. On Good Friday, the nineteenth day of bleeding, Cloretta reported bleeding from all sites simultaneously and she felt as if 'it was all over'. From that day no further bleeding took place. She was watched by her family and by members of her church closely during the Easter season a year later and except for an unsubstantiated report by one observer of some bleeding on one occasion, there was no recurrence. None of the doctors who examined her described her as a hysterical personality. She had no obvious symptoms of neurosis and the only significant history as background for the stigmata was her religiosity.

The report in the psychiatric journal said that it was her auditory hallucinations which had to be taken seriously. She talked of voices telling her to go and pray with certain people.

> She did so, believing that her prayers would have healing powers and in each case they did. It must be recalled that her family is very religious and that the child herself speaks in reverent terms about the life of Jesus and other biblical matters with which she is acquainted in detail.

Dr Lifschutz and Dr Early said the most striking psychological quality present was Cloretta's identification with the figure of Christ.

> She was also preoccupied with Christ's suffering and saw her life as dedicated to relieve suffering in others.

Cloretta's voices started a few days before the bleeding, and she heard them during her time of prayer before going to bed. She never reported seeing any visions and the voices she heard were clear and gave a simple message that her prayers would be answered. As well as reading the Bible she had also read the book *Crossroads* by John Webster. This religious book about the crucifixion made an impact on her when she read it a week before the bleeding began. Also four days before the bleeding she had watched a television programme about the crucifixion. She was much moved by it and says that that night she had had a vivid dream about the film. She denied any knowledge of the phenomenon of stigmata before she herself experienced it. Yet having heard about it and experienced it first-hand, she clearly identified herself with St Francis of Assisi. It is reported that on one occasion, during her short period of stigmatization, she was drawing pictures of St Francis and her left palm began to bleed.

The case of Cloretta Robinson is extremely unusual in that she was so young when she received the marks and in that she was a Baptist and a black American.

In the course of a journey which took him round the world in search of evidence of what he described as 'both the miraculous and the demonic', the writer John Cornwell met Georgette Faniel of Montreal, described to him by the priest who acted as his guide as 'probably the most authentic living example of a stigmatic in the world today'. A strange claim to make perhaps, but John Cornwell's description of his meeting with the seventy-four-year-old Canadian woman is worth examining.

Her religious experiences had begun at the age of six and she believed that Christ, Mary and the devil all spoke to her. When young she was a brilliant pianist, but at the age of twenty she fell ill with inexplicable paralysis and pain and for the next fifty years was virtually bedridden and, says John Cornwell, 'spent her life in constant pain and prayer. She lived an intensely private, reclusive existence.'

Like Heather Woods, Georgette has written many volumes of material which came to her in her mystical states.

One extraordinary story is told of her, that at the age of sixty-two she developed all the symptoms of pregnancy. She had taken upon herself all the discomfort of a young pregnant woman she knew, and then on the day of the birth of her friend's child, it was Georgette who suffered the pain of labour while the young woman had a trouble-free delivery.

John Cornwell admits that on hearing the story he was not encouraged to believe that all was well with Georgette. However on meeting her he describes her look of both affection and innocence, and says he was captivated from the very first moment. Her bedroom had been constructed as a shrine and was decorated with dried flowers, votive lamps and holy pictures. She told John Cornwell how Jesus spoke to her and addressed her as 'beloved . . . his little bride, his little victim of love'. She explained that the stigmata had begun in 1950 with wounds to her wrists and feet and on 25 April 1953 she had received the crown of thorns. Georgette also described a wound in her heart and how she bore the pain that Christ had suffered from carrying his cross.

As with many stigmatics Georgette described how the pain increased on Fridays and at the point of consecration during Mass.

For many years, Georgette said that, while the pain was real little evidence of injury was visible.

In 1982 she described how

on the Feast of the Precious Blood, God manifested himself with a terrible pain and by leaving a sign in my flesh in the shape of the figure two. This indicated that God and I are two in one same flesh.

The doctor who examined it said it was unbelievable and looked like luminous neon and the blood could be seen circulating. He said that the number was made up of seven dots, which Jesus has told me indicate the seven gifts of the Holy Spirit.

She told John Cornwell that Satan also spoke to her and tried to distort her prayers and told her that her whole life had been wasted in spiritual pride.

Sometimes he attacks me physically. He has tried to strangle me and bruises of his fingers have been left on my neck.

John Cornwell remained with Georgette during Mass and heard her gasping and moaning as if racked with pain. Afterwards he asked to see her wounds and examined them closely.

She allowed me to hold both of her feet one by one . . . Her feet and ankles were very badly swollen and in the centre of each foot was a distinct deep purplish mark, red and angry at the edges. The skin of the whole foot looked extremely tender and inflamed, but it was neither broken nor showed any signs of blood. It was as if the wounds had been painted on. But scrutinizing the marks very closely, the images seemed to be composed of broken or distended capillaries as a result of some trauma below the skin's surface. Both feet looked extremely painful.

Next I looked at her wrists. There were no similar vivid signs, but instead monstrous swellings that had the appearance of an unusual kind of arthritis. The skin was drawn taut almost to breaking point and although I touched the pressure area very gently she shut her eyes and gasped as if in agonizing pain.

Georgette also allowed John Cornwell to see the sign of the alliance, the number two made up of seven bright scarlet spots on her hip.

She told him:

My wounds are a great grace. It is by Christ's wounds that we are healed. There is a prayer of St John of the Cross: 'Lord wound me with the wound of love, which may be healed only by being wounded again.'

Away from Montreal reflecting on what he had seen John Cornwell pondered on how Georgette's life had seemed morbid, unhealthy and self-absorbed. Was she not a classical hysteric, he asked himself, with her voices, phantom pregnancy, dramatic dermatological signs and years of self-absorbing chronic ailments?

But he concluded not to dismiss Georgette outright with psychological or neurological explanations.

Her personality did not strike me as altogether neurotic . . . above all it seemed to me that the dedication of her life to prayer and contemplation was genuine.

What John Cornwell found difficult to understand was how in the twentieth century there were still people who felt a positive vocation to suffering and to sharing the mystery of Christ's suffering on the cross which is so central to the Christian idea of redemption. He left Montreal impressed but undecided. His visit to Georgette had been an essential part of a journey of discovery which was as much about discovering himself as it had been about uncovering evidence of the miraculous.

When a phenomenon like stigmata crosses the Atlantic from the old world to the new it remains essentially the same even though the setting might be radically different. Father Jim Bruse's church is modern and serves a wide area where only a minority of the population is Roman Catholic. The faithful arrive by car and there is a huge car park attached to the church complex. Georgette lives in a modest clapboard apartment block in downtown Montreal. Cloretta was described as coming from a lower middle-class family in West Oakland, a suburb of San Francisco. Today she lives in a typical small American town outside the conurbation and is in no way distinguished from her contemporaries by her childhood experience.

By contrast at Capodrise near Caserta in Italy the population is overwhelmingly Roman Catholic and the local people of the parish can reach the church by foot without needing to drive for miles.

Yet at Capodrise in 1991 there was also a stigmatic drawing the crowds and causing some consternation to the church authorities. Michele Improta was then a youth of eighteen. Although male, which was unusual for a stigmatist in Italy, his experience was otherwise typical for a stigmatist in a Mediterranean country. He reportedly had visions, and his hands and feet exhibited painful bleeding wounds. Local sceptics talked of mass hysteria in the town, 'self-inflicted wounds', 'tribal rituals' and 'paganism'. Nevertheless he attracted many devout people around him including a hundred supporters who formed themselves into a prayer group and protected Michele from the crowds. They dressed in a uniform consisting of a dark blue cloak and a chaplet with a picture of the Madonna.

Michele claimed he had had his first vision at the age of three when he was walking on the beach with the nuns who were then looking after him. He described later how he had seen a

> most beautiful woman, wearing white clothes and with a heavenly aura and azure blue eyes.
>
> With her right hand she signed to me to come near, then in a low voice said, 'Michele, my son, the Christ child wants you to give yourself to him, to imitate him and to serve him all your life. I will always be near you and will never leave you.'

From that moment Michele said he had always been aware of the Virgin Mary and the visions continued. The beautiful woman identified herself as the Madonna of the Rosary, the virgin of Medjugorge.

The lady behaved towards me like a mother. I was filled with joy and on the day of my first communion she accompanied me to the altar.

Michele also much later had a vision of Jesus.

He was most beautifully clothed in white and surrounded by a dazzling light. 'You will come with me to Calvary,' he said, 'suffering my same sufferings for the salvation of souls.' At that moment from his hands, his feet, from his ribs came out rays of light which pierced me in the same places and since then I have had bleeding wounds which give me terrible pain, which have terrified medical people, and which no-one has been able to explain.

As in the case of Father Bruse, Michele has talked about statues around him weeping

as if they were made of flesh and bone. From the eyes of the baby Jesus, made of plaster and kept by my bed, there came drops of blood.

In addressing pilgrims who had come to see him, from a chapel balcony Michele insisted that he himself was not sacred, although voices from the crowd called out 'Holy One!'

'It is the virgin you are near to,' Michele insisted. 'Go and give your thanks to her.'

Italian newspaper reports have said that psychiatrists have examined Michele and the ecclesiastical authorities have investigated his case but both are cautious about making any pronouncements.

Michele has said that many doctors have

> applied science to understand my wounds but they are unable to give an explanation. At the beginning even my parents thought I was mentally ill, I had a hole in my mind. They thought the phenomena were just the results of a curious fantasy, but for me it all seems normal. The psychiatrists who have examined me know that I am fully aware of what is going on.

Another contemporary case of stigmata reported by a Western journalist confirms the pattern of behaviour which emerges within a community when a case of stigmata emerges. There is a local curiosity, which either turns to devotion or derision, and an official church and medical wariness. This report was published in 1981 and was filed by UPI for American newspapers. It concerns a small town in Portugal, Escorial.

> An olive grove on the outskirts of the small hillside town is daily attracting flocks of people from the surrounding countryside. The object of their attention is Ampara Cueva, a forty-three-year-old mother of seven, who was ordered by the Blessed Virgin Mary (BVM) in a vision to recite the Rosary in public at this spot. Exactly when this initiating vision occurred is not reported, but one gathers it might have been in November 1980.

According to Francisca Herranz, the wife of a local baker, it was on a day in that month that she noticed Ampara standing entranced in her shop with drops of blood on her forehead. 'We made her sit down,' says Mrs Herranz, 'and we saw that blood was also coming out of her hands and ribs.' This stigmatic trance lasted 'almost two hours', and since then had been repeated on the major feast days of the Catholic Church, especially those falling on a Friday, the traditional day of Christ's death. In contrast to the public recitation, the stigmatic attacks are kept as private as possible, attended only by relatives and close friends, who say that most of the usual forms of traditional wounds suffered by Christ are manifested: bleeding from hands, feet, side of breast, knees, and forehead. A witness, Mrs Feliza Jeminez, claims she saw the stigmata on Good Friday 1981, when a relative of Ampara let her into the stigmatic's bedroom. She said, 'I saw her on the bed, her flesh as white and cold as marble. It's hard to believe if you don't see it with your own eyes.'

It seems that at the appropriate times Ampara enters an ecstasy during which the stigmata appear and conversations are held with BVM and Christ. The description of the stigmata is vague – at one point they are described as 'scars', and at another as 'bleeding like sweat'. The reporter met Ampara – a 'stocky, youthful' woman who works as a maid – during one of the regular 9 a.m. recitations in the olive grove to the south of the town. Replying in 'a matter-of-fact way' she said she was in other respects an ordinary person. 'As a child I had a strong feeling about the Virgin, perhaps because my mother died and I had a tough time with my stepmother. Still I was not overly religious and almost did not know how to pray.' Then she smiled: 'But I'm learning now.'

It is not possible to say exactly how many stigmatics there are in the world today. There is one pious legend that states that there are always twelve stigmatics alive at any given time, representing the twelve apostles, with the implication that when one stigmatic dies the gift is passed on to someone new. Dates of the deaths of stigmatics and the reoccurrence of the wounds in new subjects do not tally neatly, but it is the case that for the last two centuries at least the number of people at any given time with the stigmata is roughly twelve. Today, the best estimate that can be given is that there are around twenty people alive who have had the stigmata although the marks are not present in all the stigmatics at the same time. The doubt exists in that there remains at least one case in Ireland which is reported but has not yet been verified by the author and three cases known about are of elderly people who might in recent months have died.

❖

FIVE

Authentication

It is only after death that a person, about whom amazing religious stories are told, is fully investigated by the Roman Catholic Church. Often this happens when a case is put forward for a person to be canonized.

Twenty-five years after his death the cult of Padre Pio of Pietrelcina gathers momentum. Growing pressure is being put on the Vatican for the priest to be canonized. No doubt a suitable time will have had to have elapsed before this will take place, as in his day Padre Pio was a thorn in the side to the Catholic authorities. The Church put many restrictions on his ministry as his reputation as a counsellor, priest, confessor as well as stigmatic spread around Italy and the world. He was born Francesco Forgione and was the son of a peasant family in southern Italy. He was a Capuchin monk, and had joined the order in 1902.

His life is probably even now being examined in great detail by the Vatican authorities and the devil's advocate is at work finding flaws in the priest's pious reputation. But to his followers Padre Pio's life has reached legendary proportions. Padre Pio was based at St Giovanni Rotondo near Foggia and he carried the marks, it is said, for fifty years. Although towards the end of his life his marks began to fade and were far less active and at his death the wounds were not visible at all. However at the height of their activity it is said they seeped a cup of blood a day. He lived the austere life of his particular Franciscan order starting each day with Mass and spending much time hearing confessions. Hundreds of stories are told by visitors who claim that after just a few words or even a glance from the friar it felt as if he had seen into their soul and they found the solution to their problems or the seat of their guilt. There are no stories of Padre Pio having survived without food but it is said he ate very sparingly for a man of his build.

His marks had originally appeared in 1918. The image to which he was particularly dedicated at that time was a horrific one of the crucifixion and after a period of meditation in front of the statue it is said that Padre Pio let out a tremendous cry in the church and his brother monks coming to his aid saw for the first time the wounds on his hands and feet. Nowhere was there evidence of the wounds having been self-inflicted and for the many years they remained open they never became septic. The events of that day spread around the world and in 1920 the *Daily Mail* ran an article about what it described as extraordinary scenes at St Giovanni Rotondo.

The peasants refuse to confess to any but the young friar or to receive Communion from another's hand, and in consequence the rest of the monastery is idle, while long queues besiege the young Franciscan and gaze in wonder at the markings on his hands and sandalled feet . . .

What alarmed the Vatican authorities was not so much the marks on his hands and feet but the fact that he was the centre of a personality cult. A whole range of associated phenomena were attributed to him including healing powers, the feat of bilocation, his ability to create a mysterious perfume, and his amazing perception of the human mind.

Two examples of his supernatural gifts illustrate the nature of the claims that were made about him. One concerns an American bombing mission during the Second World War. As he was approaching Foggia the squadron leader saw ahead of him, in the clouds, the figure of a monk holding up his hands and gesturing him to turn back. The squadron leader turned back and jettisoned his bombs. On reporting the account to his commanding officer, the squadron leader was, not unexpectedly, hospitalized. The plan was to send him home on special medical leave.

Naturally the airman was very worried that his imagination could have played him such tricks, but while in hospital he learnt from an Italian orderly that in the region there lived a monk with extraordinary powers.

After the war the squadron leader made some inquiries and heard about Padre Pio. He went to see him and to his surprise and reassurance found that he recognized the monk. He was convinced that it was Padre Pio he had seen in the clouds those years before.

And the second story is told in the book *The Friar of St Giovanni* by John McCaffery and it goes like this:

An Italian writer and broadcaster was subject to severe migraine attacks. On one occasion, just prior to a broadcast, he was in desperation, both with the pain and the thought that he could not proceed with the programme. As he lay on the couch resting and hoping the attack would pass, he was suddenly aware of Padre Pio standing over him. The monk laid his hand on his head and then disappeared. The migraine was cured.

A few days later the broadcaster went to see Padre Pio.

'Well Giovanni,' he was asked, 'and how is the head?'

'Thank you Padre,' Giovanni replied, 'very well indeed.'

'Ah,' said Padre Pio, smiling as though at a joke they had in common, 'those hallucinations!'

In 1919 Padre Pio was examined by Professor A. Bignami, a pathologist and diagnostic from the Roman university. Father Herbert Thurston, one of the Church's leading experts on mysticism, reported the examination in this way in *The Physical Phenomena of Mysticism*:

Although some difficulty was caused by the fact that Padre Pio, at that date, had been using iodine as an astringent to check the bleeding, and that the marks in consequence might have been judged by a careless observer to be merely the stain of iodine, Professor Bignami attests to the existence of superficial scars upon the hands and feet and the form of a cross upon the left breast. He finds that these points are marked by extreme sensitiveness (hyperaesthesia) and does not consider them to have been artificially produced. The lesions are described by him as due to a necrosis of the epidermis of neurotic origin and their symmetrical arrangement he considers to be probably attributable to unconscious suggestion. In his view there is nothing in the case which cannot be fully accounted for by natural causes.

The crucial part of the professor's findings is that he is convinced the marks had not been deliberately and fraudulently self-inflicted. Like two other open-minded physicians before him, who had looked generally at the subject of stigmata, Dr Dumas of the Sorbonne writing in 1907 and Dr Pierre Janet writing in 1901 in the *Bulletin of the International Institute of Psychology*, he did not try to dismiss the visual evidence but rather he attempted to construct a natural hypothesis to explain it.

Only one official photograph of Padre Pio's hands exists. It was taken after the priest had been medically examined under orders from his superiors. The photograph was attested as genuine by an Italian commissioner for oaths. The doctors who saw Padre Pio, however, could not agree on how the wounds were caused. In 1968, in the course of producing a television documentary about Padre Pio, the BBC sent all available medical evidence to a London physician specializing in psychological medicine. He was not a Roman Catholic but had taken a special interest in physical symptoms associated with psychological conditions. He produced this guarded explanation.

If we imagine the Franciscan friar on the day of the commemoration of the stigmatization of the founder of his order, St Francis, rapt in prayer, focusing his whole mind on the saint, perhaps striving to identify with him; if we remember that Padre Pio has often been seen in trance-like states, we must ask ourselves: 'Could these wounds be caused by autosuggestion or by self-hypnosis?'

The second possibility is that the wounds were self-inflicted. Now to say that a person wounds himself, is not necessarily to say that he is a swindler or a charlatan. I myself, and some of my colleagues, have seen people who have shown the five wounds, believing them to be stigmatization, but in all these cases, it has been finally proved that they have been self-inflicted, although the person might have been quite unaware of this fact.

Well, this then is the case of the devil's advocate. The two possibilites: autosuggestion and self-mutilation. How convincing is this case? I have discussed the evidence with a number of colleagues who are very eminent in this field, and there are a number of features of the wounds of Padre Pio which are inexplicable to me. I can find no account of bleeding being produced either by hypnosis or autosuggestion. It is most remarkable that wounds which have been self-inflicted should not show signs of reddening, inflammation, infection or signs of healing over a prolonged period. As a psychiatrist, I must remain in a state of profound uncertainty.

While there is no suggestion that Padre Pio himself encouraged the mass adulation which was to accompany him, it was he who suffered the admonishments of the Church.

By way of giving him a psychiatric reference, Professor Bignami, who examined Padre Pio in 1919, said that apart from the evidence of the lesions themselves, Padre Pio exhibited no hysterical symptoms. He is described as being always exceptionally calm and composed. He said that he never suffered from any nervous maladies. He had never been subject to fainting fits, convulsions or tremors. He said he slept well and was not troubled with dreams. This however said that he had amazing control over his body and that in October 1925 when he had to be operated on for a hernia he refused an anaesthetic. Later he turned down the skills of an anaesthetist when a second operation had to be performed, this time for the removal of a cyst. Interestingly St Francis is said to have endured a cauterization from a red-hot iron, performed by a medieval physician, with amazing stoicism. It is said that St Francis spoke to the fire in which the iron for the cauterization was being heated, and said 'My brother fire, noble and useful among all other creatures, be kindly to me in this hour.'

Very soon after his stigmatization the Church authoritatively stated that Padre Pio was a man of remarkable sanctity. To quote Montigue Summers in his book, like Thurson's study also called *The Physical Phenomena of Mysticism*:

Miracles had been worked by his intercession; his ecstasies were frequent and prolonged: several instances, proved beyond all doubt, of bilocation were recorded.

In 1922 the Archbishop of Simla, writing in the *Simla Times*, gave an account of his interview with Padre Pio.

> The stigmata came all at once like a sudden and unexpected blow, during his thanksgiving after Mass.
>
> The marks on the hand are like dried blood. In the palm the perforation is perfectly circular with the rays of dried blood going from one side to the other, and is about the size of a penny. It looks much redder than the palm. It is precisely as if a big nail had been driven right up to its head into the palm, and the point has come out on the other side where a hole is, which can be seen quite clearly, covered with a pink skin.

The Vatican authorized a medical inquiry and it is said that on one occasion during the medical investigation the clinical thermometer used proved unable to register the high temperature of Padre Pio's body, and was broken by the abnormal expansion of the mercury in the tube. This suggestion that some stigmatics, or others prone to what is described as mystical phenomena, can exhibit an extraordinarily high body temperature, is not unique.

In an attempt to spare Padre Pio the pressure of publicity and the demands of the crowds, the Vatican declared that all pilgrimages to Padre Pio must cease. Padre Pio was not himself censured, but the Vatican made the ruling to protect him.

But the Vatican's call was not heeded and was repeated in 1924. And those who had not conformed to the Vatican's instructions were refused permission to write to Padre Pio for mystical instruction and for him to reply.

Padre Pio began to say Mass at an extraordinarily early hour of the morning in order to discourage sightseers, and the devout, eager to see evidence of his stigmata as he celebrated the Eucharist.

Montigue Summers reflecting on the church authorities' attitude to Padre Pio said, 'The way of the mystic is hard. It is not a path of flowers, but of thorns.'

A contemporary of Padre Pio was the Bavarian, Therese Neumann. She was born eleven years later, in 1898, and died six year earlier in 1962. She too attracted much attention and was subjected to the most intense scrutiny. In contrast to the quiet contemplative life of Padre Pio, dedicated to the celebration of the Mass and the hearing of confessions, and in no way willing to become a public display, Therese Neumann could almost be said to have encouraged the tales of her extraordinary deeds. She received wounds, had visions and is even attributed with bilocation but the photographs of her lying in a bloodstained bed, with tears of blood streaming down her cheeks, reliving a Good Friday passion, are grotesque in the extreme. The chances of her being seriously considered, let alone accepted, for canonization are remote, but her story is worth telling as in her day she attracted every bit as much public interest as her contemporary Padre Pio.

In 1918, Therese injured her back when carrying buckets of water during an attempt to put out a house fire in the village where she worked. From that moment onwards her health went into decline. She became incontinent and was hospitalized. She suffered convulsions and at one stage it is said she lost her sight temporarily. She also had a range of other symptoms, including temporary paralysis and an inability to speak for a period of time which would appear from the descriptions to be of a psychiatric rather than physical nature. Then quite remarkably in 1923 Therese Neumann's sight was restored after praying to the Blessed Therese of Lisieux. Word of the miraculous cure spread around the district of Konnersreuth. Although her sight was restored many of the other physical problems remained. Two years later when Therese of Lisieux was canonized a second miracle cure occurred and Therese Neumann's other physical symptoms were reversed. She told everyone that she had heard a voice asking if she wished to be cured and had seen a bright light. But her medical problems continued, even though she was now able to walk. At one time it was feared she had an appendicitis after she complained of pain. And then on the night of 4th May she had a vision of Christ in the garden of the Mount of Olives. She saw Jesus as he knelt there and suddenly felt a pain in her side. She then became aware of blood running down her side and a wound which had opened up in her side continued to bleed until the next day. In the weeks that followed Therese again experienced the vision and also saw Christ being whipped, mocked and given the crown of thorns. In one of her visions too she is said to have seen Christ carrying the cross to Calvary. By Holy Week of 1926 she had had a series of visions of Jesus' passion and exhibited on her body a full set of stigmata.

Therese Neumann's case received much publicity and scepticism. She was closely examined by doctors and by church representatives. In particular her long abstinence from food was investigated. While no-one ever came up with any direct evidence of fraudulent activity a question of doubt always remained. There was no way of proving definitively that Therese Neumann was not illicitly eating food or mutilating herself in order to attract attention. It was even suspected that her family, which benefited from the notoriety, connived in this.

That is not to say that her visions of the Passion and her initial marking were not genuine, in the sense that they were a psychosomatic manifestation. Clearly however Therese Neumann was a very disturbed person.

As was Teresa Musco who was a stigmatized mystic who lived near Naples and who died in 1976. Yet her reputation is such that her case for canonization is now being processed and her local priest, Father Franco, keeps her home as it was in her lifetime for visitors to come and see. He also has a photograph album which shows Teresa in states of religious ecstasy with blood trickling down her face and close-up shots of her stigmata in full flow. There is even a picture demonstrating how in Teresa's case the stigmata took the form of a hole right through the hand. It shows her hand held up against the window with the light shining through. Teresa's statues and religious portraits, which reputedly wept blood, remain uncleaned.

Teresa had endured bad health throughout her life and had over a hundred surgical operations. At the end of her life her kidneys failed and before her death at the age of thirty-three she had a period on dialysis and a transplant operation.

It has not come as a surprise to many Roman Catholics that despite her local parish priest's devotion to her cause, the Vatican is taking its time to evaluate her case. For as Amanda Mitchison wrote in the *Independent Magazine* in 1991,

many liberal Roman Catholics find it hard to accept Teresa's self-mortifying, masochist brand of Catholicism.

She referred to herself as a 'dungheap', a 'little worm covered in mud', a 'crumb of dirt'. 'Lord use me as your cleaning rag!' was a favourite exhortation in her diary. There is also something very southern Italian about Teresa's apparitions, with the trio of Madonna, Christ and baby Jesus forming a substitute for her own nightmarish family. In Teresa's diary Christ comes over as domineering, and the Madonna as petulant and fatalistic: 'I appeared in Portugal,' the Madonna told Teresa, 'giving messages and nobody listened to me. And at Lourdes and La Salette only a few hard hearts saw the light . . . Fire and smoke will take over the world . . . The water of the ocean will become fire and vapour. Foam will rise up, cover Europe and bury everything . . .'

Meanwhile, the statue of baby Jesus was forever seeking attention. Father Franco remembers: 'Quite often when we were eating a frugal meal, baby Jesus, lying in the other room, would start to emit tears, and he would have to be taken and put at the head of the table. At other times Teresa would be going out in the car and she would realize she had forgotten something and turn back. She would find the statue crying and then we would take him with us.'

Such curious behaviour might weigh against Teresa when the case for her canonization is considered. For the Roman Catholic Church, although prepared to accept the miraculous does occur, is always reluctant to be seen to condone curious and excessive religious behaviour. If it does it is only after a number of centuries have elapsed. Stigmatization is no evidence, in the Vatican's eyes, of the special qualities which can result in the accolade of canonization. The Church believes also in counterfeit stigmata, the signs of crucifixion being produced by the devil to tempt the recipient with the sin of pride or to mock them. Stigmatics themselves talk of what they believe to be encounters with the devil.

Monsignor Albert Farges in his book *The Mystical Phenomena* wrote:

it is certain that the wicked angel can, at will . . . produce fantastic scenes in our minds which come from his suggestion.

He then continued to give an authoritative view of the Roman Catholic Church's approach to distinguishing between what it considers divine and what it considers diabolic mystical phenomena.

Even if the devil should provoke heavenly images of our Lord, the Blessed Virgin or the saints and heavenly joys, or else infernal images of spectres, devils, infinite despair or the most seductive pictures of human passion, there will be no revelation, no prophecy, nothing transcendental, nothing that we could not have imagined for ourselves in a moment of fever or exaltation . . . The diabolical vision begins by bringing joy, a sense of safety and sweetness and ends in anxiety, sadness, fear and disgust.

The Roman Catholic Church does nevertheless accept that the stigmata can be genuine and can be a gift from God. Yet this point of view raises a number of difficult theological questions. In particular, why should God wish to intercede in earthly affairs in this manner and why should he have only started doing so in the thirteenth century? If the stigmata is seen as some kind of divine party trick to inspire and encourage the faithful, it is curious that for the first twelve hundred years of Christendom the trick was never played.

The phenomenon cannot be explained away in simple terms and one part of understanding its nature is to examine its origins.

SIX

Why Then?

The sudden appearance of the stigmata in the thirteenth century would appear at first sight to be a curious event, even to those who readily accept the miraculous. Why should it be that after over twelve centuries in which such a phenomenon was never even contemplated that there should be an on-rush of cases? It could be supposed that once the idea had been set in motion others consciously or unconsciously copied the pattern of St Francis. But mimicry is unlikely to be a complete answer. At the time there was no system of instant communication and news of St Francis' experience would have taken a while to reach all parts of Europe. And yet the subsequent cases of stigmata occurred very soon after St Francis' vision and marking and there were even cases of people bearing the wounds of crucifixion which, although possibly self-inflicted, coincided with the marking of the famous saint.

Indeed twelve years before the stigmatization of St Francis the Blessed Mary of Oignes is said, in a near contemporary biography, to have had a similar experience after intense contemplation of the passion. She is said to have experienced such intense visions of the suffering of Christ, wounds were detected on her body when it was washed at her death. The wounds corresponded with those of crucifixion. At this distance of time, however, it is not possible to determine whether the wounds were self-inflicted as an act of empathetic piety, or whether the wounds appeared without apparent external physical cause. If, in the case of the Blessed Mary the wounds were self-inflicted, as are the scourge wounds of those who submit to the extreme religious penance of flagellation, it would not be right to conclude they were fraudulent. As it appears she never drew attention to the marks in her lifetime, there was clearly no intent to deceive. Fraud only arises when a person carrying the stigmata claims they are supernatural when in fact they have been knowingly self-inflicted. It was also said of the Blessed Mary that she could miraculously see the Blessed Sacrament and in doing this she had a claim to mysticism in common with a number of subsequent stigmatics.

An answer to the question as to why stigmata appeared as a phenomenon at this particular time in medieval Europe lies less in mimicry and more in the way in which there was a re-emphasis of certain parts of the faith. Between the different Churches and at different times within the same Church, the mysteries of faith are not lent equal weight. In some times and in some Churches the role of the Virgin Mary is made central, while in other Churches it is the apocalyptic prophecies of the Book of Revelation and elsewhere which are emphasized most vigorously. Around the thirteenth century, it was the nature of God as a human being and the consequent suffering of that human body on the cross which many pious believers came to concentrate on. In some ways it was a reaction by devout believers against some of the prevailing attitudes of the Church of the day which was becoming lax and worldly. There was too a question of authority. Those who in their piety wished to have direct experience and communion with the suffering body of Christ could only do so with the approval of the Church. In other words they only had access to the body of Christ at Mass through the priest celebrating the Mass. Lay people, especially women, relied entirely on the Church for access to the thing they held most precious. They had thus to seek the authority, mediation or permission of the Church to have contact with the body of Jesus. So it was that at that time through prayer, meditation, austere living and even direct self-infliction of pain, certain pious and holy people attempted to bypass that route to Christ which involved the approval of a church with which they felt unhappy. They began to suffer with him and like him in their own bodies.

Further evidence of the spiritual upheaval of the time can be seen in a study of the art of the period which gradually became more graphic in its representations of Christ's sufferings. With the new emphasis being placed on the contemplation of the Passion of Christ and the reality of the incarnation, religious paintings began to show blood pouring from wounds and the real agony of that cruel method of execution, the crucifixion. In earlier times pictures had been far more symbolic.

It is also the case that after St Francis the stigmata was seen as a predominantly female experience. It was naturally assumed that more women carried the marks than men because women are more prone to 'hysterical' behaviour. But the explanation is not that obvious for indeed if women are intrinsically more emotional, imaginative, religious or hysterical than men why did it take twelve centuries of Christianity for these traits to emerge?

An explanation perhaps lies in looking at the structure of the Church. In her study of the spirituality of the High Middle Ages, *Jesus as Mother*, Caroline Walker Bynum writes:

> The first five hundred years of Christianity had established that a male clergy, whose authority was based on office, would serve as the fundamental channel of God's message and God's grace to the laity – that is all men (including monks) who were not clergy and all women. But despite the continuing importance of ecclesiastical office, the early Middle Ages have frequently been seen as the period of 'monastic spirituality', both in the sense that monks were the vicarious worshippers for all of society and in the sense that the monastic role was held up to all as the Christian ideal. To ordinary people in the ninth and tenth centuries contact with the clergy was often limited to baptism, burial and paying tithes . . . Salvation, for oneself and one's relatives, came by making gifts to monks and nuns who said the prayers that assured a right relationship to God . . . The most significant locations of holiness and supernatural power were the relics of saints. It was the Gregorian Reform movement of the mid eleventh century that created a Church headed by the clergy

and began the process of locating supernatural power most centrally in the Eucharist, which the priest controlled.

While the priest had control, there was nevertheless a growing demand from the laity for involvement. The devotion to the Eucharist grew in the last quarter of the twelfth century and more of the laity were eager to see the host at the moment of consecration. This gave communicants a direct feeling of contact with the humanity of Christ. In 1264 Pope Urban IV ordered the Church to observe the Feast of Corpus Christi, the body of Christ. The history of this feast can be traced to the vision of St Juliana, a Prioress from Liège in 1246. Corpus Christi is the feast which involves the veneration of the Blessed Sacrament. The 'miraculous' properties of the body of Christ were firmly believed in at this time and it was believed that strength could be drawn from simply looking at the host, and it was often the practice for a dying person to have the sacrament held in front of their eyes.

The eleventh and twelfth centuries had been a time of general religious revival in Europe. Individuals became increasingly interested in having an experience of God for themselves rather than through the mediation of the institutions of the Church, whether monastic or clerical. While by the twelfth and early thirteenth centuries there was not yet a sense that individuals could seek their own experience and salvation, a sufficient spirit of individualism had evolved for new groups to develop. These often developed away from the church structures. They were groups within which individuals could discover themselves and the inner mysteries of their relationship with God. There was a rise in the numbers of women seeking a religious life. One of the reasons for this was that at that period in history, there were in the population more women than men. In addition many of the men were abroad fighting the Crusades and those who did not return left widows. An idea gained ground that as an alternative to marriage, virginity was a high calling and a source of spiritual power. Conditions were right for a growth in women's religious movements.

There was both an expansion of convents and of new lay religious communities such as the Beguines. Women who joined the latter took no vows but dedicated their lives to an exploration of their own spirituality. In particular this took the form of a devotion to the Eucharist and the humanity of Christ concentrated in an exploration of an intense contemplation of the physical sufferings of Christ. They began to seek to experience the suffering of Christ for themselves as if in imitation. And the ultimate imitation of Christ was to share the wounds.

These new independent religious and members of new communities had thus bypassed their need for the inter-cessions of the Church. The Church could not disapprove of their piety and yet could do nothing but acknowledge that in pursuing this piety there was a reduced role for the priests. Of course this new emphasis on individual piety was open to the priests themselves to pursue, but they, through the celebration of the Mass, already had their direct line to God. It was therefore a movement of particular interest to the laity, especially women, who were specifically excluded from the priesthood.

However individualism had not developed so far that a breakaway from the authority of the Church was implied. The focus of individual devotion remained the Eucharist. The Church therefore had some veto and could deny the sacraments as it did in the mid thirteenth century when the Chapter of the Abbey of Citeaux in France agreed to forbid communion to those who could not retain their senses during the celebration of the Mass. Clearly there were individuals at the time whose devotions were so excessive that they experienced ecstasies at the point of communicating.

Yet the fact that the Church had a veto carried with it the implication that any excessive religious behaviour, which did not attract its stated disapproval, was thereby condoned and confirmed by the Church.

So it was that in the thirteenth century, at the time when the first cases of stigmata surfaced, a situation existed whereby lay people could explore their deep inner spirituality and personal relationships with God under the protection and control, if not always the encouragement, of the Church. Thus there emerged in much of Europe groups of people about whom stories were told of their particular devotion to the pursuit of mysticism. Francis of Assisi was such a person. He was unusual in that as a man he preferred not to exercise the option of priesthood. But in the main, because the priesthood was not open to women, the new emphasis on individual spirituality, the suffering of Christ, through a devotion to the Eucharist, was largely female.

As Caroline Walker Bynum put it

the psychological and spiritual reasons for this female concentration on the Eucharist seem to have been fundamentally the same as the reasons for the flowering of women's mysticism – this is, the need for a substitute for clerical experience. If Christ was incarnated in the hands of the celebrating priest as in the Virgin's womb, might he not also be incarnated within the communicating nun or Beguine, and might not each of these types of spiritual maternity bear fruit in spiritual children?

Devotion and an ardent love for the humanity and passion of Christ often, at this time, took the form of visions and rapture associated with the veneration of the body of Christ. St Christina of Stommeln, who received the stigmata in 1268, is said to have viewed the Eucharist as a perpetual commemoration of her marriage to the heavenly bridegroom. If, as the Church taught in marriage, two people became as one flesh her devotion to Christ necessarily took a physical form. Also, if sin is the separation from God, it follows that a sinner's salvation is in seeking the closest possible identification with God and the very closest possible identification is to empathize totally with the wounds of his suffering on earth. In the case of St Christina there is possible evidence that her wounds were both spontaneously occurring and enhanced by physical means. For if the mechanism whereby the body produces the stigmata, whatever its ultimate source, is dermatological it would follow that only the skin would show evidence of the marks. However St Christina's preserved skull shows markings and indentations supposedly corresponding to a crown of thorns.

Without doubt the 'supernatural and divine' wounds of the pious women of the time were enhanced by physical action. Elizabeth of Herkenrode re-enacted the whole passion every twenty-four hours in the course of which she struck herself fearful blows and, as mentioned earlier, Lukardis of Oberweimar had the habit of driving her fingernails into her palms as well as being prone to repeated ecstasies and receiving the stigmata.

A good account of the Cistercian nun of Herkenrode near Liège was made around the year 1275 by the Abbot of Clairvaux. He was rather sceptical about the claims being made about the nun who supposedly re-enacted the violent scenes of suffering of Christ on a regular daily basis, beginning in the middle of the night with the arrest and ending at Compline with the body of Christ being placed in the tomb. However Abbot Philip met Elizabeth and saw the violent act for himself.

> Stretching out her arm and raising her fist threateningly, she would strike herself a violent blow on the jaw so that her whole body seemed to reel and totter under the impact . . . at other stages she would be writhing, as it seemed, in agony upon the floor, beating her head against the ground over and over again.

It was a spectacle which greatly impressed the onlookers.

Abbot Philip also made a close examination of the stigmata on the nun's feet, hands and side. He saw blood spurting from the wounds, from her eyes and from beneath her nails.

The devotions to the Eucharist by women of the time resulted in a number of appearances of the stigmata. Examples of cases about which no suggestion of fraud or self-mutilation have been made, include three women who have been venerated, the Blessed Angela of Foligno, the Blessed Vanna of Orvieto, a Dominican of the Third Order and the Blessed Helen of Veszprim, a member of a strictly enclosed Dominican convent in Hungary.

The suggestion that the stigmata occurred at this time as a result of the new forms of devotion in which women had a particular interest is not the entire explanation as to why, once the stigmata had occurred, it was to recur again and again. It might be too simple to suggest that there was mimicry involved but without doubt later stigmatics were inspired by the stories they heard of the earlier ones. The Blessed Helen of Veszprim, for instance, was stigmatized first on October 4th (the Feast of St Francis), little more than ten years after the death of the saint. And it certainly must be the case that in the regions where cases have recurred most frequently the latest stigmatics, even if they have not been mimicking their forebears, have at least been inspired by their example. There are instances where individuals who have shared a name with an outstanding mystic or stigmatic of the past have been particularly inspired by that mystic's example. It is said of Therese Neumann, the controversial twentieth-century stigmatic, that one of her earlier experiences of being 'miraculously' healed occurred on 17 May 1925, the day that in Rome her namesake from Lisieux was being canonized.

The visions and ecstasies which accompanied the medieval devotion to the Eucharist and could result in stigmata are not substantially different from the visions reported by other women in subsequent years. The sharing of the suffering, the visionary feeling herself to be crucified, was described by Ethel Chapman in the twentieth century. The cradling of the baby Jesus was described by Jane Hunt.

The purpose however to which the ecstasies, mysticisms and devotions were put in the thirteenth century was more particular to its age. The religious women of the time became well known for their counsel, spiritual advice and wisdom. They wrote of their mystical experiences, composed prayers and translated and interpreted Scripture.

Their calling was to 'the cure of souls' and 'preaching', very much the same as the vocation of a priest. They were seen as channels of information which came directly from Christ and direct channels of Grace and forgiveness which supplemented, and sometimes replaced, the sacraments and the priesthood. They exercised a priestly role in all but name even though they were specifically excluded by the male-dominated Church from the priesthood. To do this they had to demonstrate an authority which both superseded that of the Church and yet could not be denied by the Church.

This authority derived from a devotion to that which was in the gift of the Church, namely the Eucharist, but a devotion which took such a form and intensity that the devotee, through visions, raptures and ultimately stigmata, could be seen to be having direct communion with God. While the Church could on occasions attempt to dampen down excess, it could not deny the piety of the women involved or the visible sign of God's supernatural favour, the stigmata.

It can thus be argued that stigmata as a phenomenon appeared on the scene as a consequence of the Church's elevation of the Eucharist; that lay people, particularly women, discovered through a personal devotion to the Eucharist a ministry every bit as valid as the priesthood; that this personal devotion was intense and mystical and centred on creating an empathy with Christ's passion; and that in certain cases the stigmata appeared as a consequence of (or as then argued a reward for) this intense concentration on the sufferings of Christ. The stigmata, appearing to be supernatural in origin, was taken as a sign of God's favour, thus reinforcing the mystical ministry.

Most men, however, had no need to follow this path. Those who wished to partake in a celebration or contemplation of the incarnation and humanity of Christ had the priesthood open to them. Until the case of Padre Pio in the twentieth century there is no reported case of a priest receiving bleeding stigmata. Although it was a man, Francis of Assisi, who was, it is generally said, the first recipient of stigmata, it is significant that he was not a priest and had opted for the mystical and visionary approach.

In medieval times, centuries before universal literacy, it was the Church which preserved and maintained the traditions of learning and literature. Yet frequently the outstanding women of the age who were also known as mystics or stigmatics were the sources of much inspirational writing. Even today such people as Heather Woods continue to be prolific authors of prayer, prophecy and mystical material, often written in an automatic, semiconscious or spiritual state.

The Church was also the patron of the arts in medieval times. It can be seen from the stories of the modern stigmatics that the religious imagery with which the recipients of the marks were familiar helped determine the nature of their experience and the form their wounds took.

The importance of the imagery in determining the exact nature of wounds in a stigmatic, or his or her other mystical experiences, is well illustrated by the case of Jane Hunt. Important to her has been her identification with the holy family, and she has used images derived from a church window she knew as a child.

In medieval times people were familiar with wall paintings, windows and carvings depicting a whole range of Bible stories. As the concentration on the incarnation developed, together with an emphasis on the sufferings of Christ, so the religious paintings of the time became more graphic in their detail. Also religious artists began to paint not just Bible stories but scenes from the lives of saints, often recent ones. The life of St Francis of Assisi became well known. Thus images of the saint were painted to show not only his empathy with the animal world but also the scene of his stigmatization by the winged seraph. Thus religious art both grew out of the religious climate of the day and helped reinforce it. And it was from within this religious climate, from the thirteenth century onwards, that the stigmatics emerged.

Why Then?

> While the Eastern Church emphasized the transfiguration and the fact that God was the light of the world, the Western Church emphasized the crucifixion, bleeding hearts, gibbets and the dark night of the soul.

The writer, a former nun and most recently the author of a book called *A History of God*, Karen Armstrong is perhaps oversimplifying the case, but her observation has a recognizable ring of truth. And the stigmata, a consequence of this emphasis on suffering and agony, is a phenomenon of the Western Church and hardly known in the east.

This point made by Karen Armstrong can be reinforced by looking further at the world of religious art. The iconographers of the Orthodox tradition have a very stylized way of representing Christ. Not for them the huge canvases or altar backdrops, or stained-glass windows of their opposite numbers in the West displaying imagined scenes of glory and pain. Yet the depiction of suffering in religious art only emerged in the West in the eleventh, twelfth and thirteenth centuries to coincide with the new theological emphasis of the Church. Even as late as the twelfth century artists avoided showing Christ in agony. He was normally shown with his body free from pain and his eyes alert and open. A closer examination of pictures of the crucifixion would even show a board placed beneath Christ's feet to guard against the full painful excesses of the full weight of the body being ripped by the nails, on the feet and hands. But by the thirteenth century it became far more common to see pictures of Christ in his dying moments or already dead, with blood pouring from the wound in his side. The use of one nail to hold both feet produced in Christ a twisting motion to heighten the image of suffering.

Art was largely dictated by the Church and the move towards depicting Christ in this way was to state a point of theology, that the incarnate Christ had suffered immeasurably. And once artists were given a free rein to depict agony there was no holding back. By the later medieval times bloody stripes and cries of anguish were also depicted.

It could be argued that an element which needs to be in place before stigmatists can produce their wounds is a tradition of art in which Christ's suffering is vividly portrayed. As in the case of Ethel Chapman whose own vision of crucifixion, the vision during which her wounds appeared, is based on the images in an illustrated Bible which she'd been given, so the medieval stigmatics produced wounds in themselves which corresponded to the pictures of Christ suffering around them. It is interesting that in more recent times, in which it has been generally accepted that the nails of crucifixion were hammered through the wrists and not the palms of the hands, modern stigmatics have produced marks on the wrist. Father Jim Bruse in the United States produced wrist wounds very much in line with modern medical thinking and the imagery of the Turin Shroud which had until recently been an important twentieth-century icon since its extraordinary image was highlighted by photography in the last century.

Thus it is that images, art, theological emphasis and

fashion have all played a part in the history of stigmata. An explanation for the phenomenon does not lie simply in the medical psychosomatic model or in believing that it is all a result of divine intervention. Neither too should the explanation be sought simply in examining the experiences of individual people. Anyone who receives the marks must be seen within a wider context of the times and communities in which they live.

❖

SEVEN

Finding One's Own Conclusion

If it can be argued that the stigmatics receive their wounds not as a supernatural divine gift but as a psychosomatic reaction to a religious experience, it makes the whole problem of understanding stigmata much easier for the twentieth-century mind. But to be entirely satisfied with that point of view one has to ignore, or somehow explain away, all the associated mystical events. Is it possible to ignore reports of saints who have levitated, miraculous healings, bilocation and the whole gamut of strange happenings and stories associated with the stigmatics of the past?

There is now no way of being able to test the accuracy of the reports of the medieval chroniclers and hagiographers. Yet their accounts of curious events cannot be easily dismissed as so much medieval superstition, for what they describe has its echoes in the twentieth century. George H. in Glasgow finds it impossible to eat properly. The medieval annals contain many stories of mystics unable to eat or surviving for long periods of time on nothing but the Eucharist. Today medical science intervenes and George is kept alive by liquid food being poured directly into his stomach via a tube. In the past his condition, seen by current medical people as an eating disorder, might have been interpreted, by pious witnesses, as a miraculous ability to live without food.

Again in the twentieth century there is the evidence of members of Father Bruse's congregation. They talk of seeing bleeding and weeping statues, the existence of which appears to have been substantiated by some hardnosed journalists. Jane Hunt and Ethel Chapman describe visions, and there is no reason to suppose that they are not telling the truth as they recall their experiences, of being transported to the Holy Land or seeing the Virgin Mary.

So if the twentieth-century cases of stigmata, which can be closely examined by an open-minded inquirer, appear to substantiate the reports of an earlier age, can it not therefore be concluded that these additional mystical phenomena are genuine? But that raises the question, what is genuine? To say that such a phenomenon is genuine is not to say that it is supernatural.

The events need to be examined from a number of perspectives. The way in which stories, myths and legends develop is important to the understanding of the reports of mystical phenomena, as is an understanding of the way in which people act and think *en masse*. It is crucial too to see how an individual's or group's willingness to accept the miraculous plays an important part. Or to put it crudely, someone who believes in miracles is more likely to witness a miracle than someone who does not believe, for he or she is more prone to interpreting a normal, but unusual, event, in terms of the miraculous.

In all probability, since the early days of human society, stories and legends have been told which have been relayed as fact, but which were not based on real events. They would, however, have been powerful stories which people wanted to believe as true, as they expressed their hidden fears and worries. There has been much speculation about the nature of these legends. Do we have a collective consciousness from which these stories emerge generation after generation? The stories differ according to the age in which they are told, but they have a similar common thread. They are stories of endless fascination, and in recent times have become the basis of novels and films.

It is possibly a human need to have a set of stories which express common fears. Similarly, might it be equally possible that stories of miracles need to exist to express human hope? These stories have an added credibility if they can be connected to a particular person or rooted in a place.

In the summer of 1985 stories emerged from the small village of Ballinspittle, in County Cork in the Republic of Ireland, that a statue of the Virgin Mary in a roadside grotto had appeared to move. As the summer passed, more and more people reported seeing the statue move, and sightings of moving Madonnas were reported from other parts of Ireland. By September there had been over thirty similar stories, many of which had been embellished to include statues which not only moved but raised their arms, talked and even walked. Enormous crowds gathered at the grottoes to see the phenomena, and one night alone at Ballinspittle a crowd of 15,000 was reported, and sixty-two buses were counted parked in the lanes.

The crowds gathered in a sloping field opposite the

grotto, and people stood there in the dark murmuring the Rosary, accompanying the sound of a prayer leader over a makeshift loudspeaker.

All eyes were on the statue, which was between three and four feet tall and set in a small, well-tended garden. It was lit by a halo of lightbulbs. From time to time someone in the crowd would exclaim, 'She moved!' and describe excitedly to his or her neighbours what the statue had just appeared to do. These were not movements which everyone saw at the same time, but it appeared that most people saw some movement at some point. Collectively, however, the effect was that the crowd were seeing a statue move, and in that form the story was told later to friends and inquirers.

Yet the fact that people saw the statue move in their own way and at their own time would suggest that the movement was not the product of an inanimate object acting in some strange physical manner, but was more to do with the way the various people looking at the statue were reacting to it. A team from the Department of Applied Psychology at University College, Cork, examined the events and explained them in this way, having carried out experiments which showed how people in the dark move and sway unwittingly.

When people weren't given visual contact with their environment then their movements were a lot less controlled and they weren't able to stay still, and moved and swayed about a lot. So what could be happening at Ballinspittle is that when you are there at twilight, you haven't got visual contact with your immediate surroundings. As is usual you are going to start swaying about on your feet, perhaps your neck will start trembling as you might have been looking up for too long, and on the back of your eye you will see the image of that little lit statue on top of the hill. You will see that image moving. Because people are not aware that it is themselves who are moving, they will interpret that movement as being the statue.

Yet how might this explain reports of other events associated with the statue? One man described how the Virgin Mary's face miraculously changed to that of Christ, and others have reported seeing her cloak blow out. The University College, Cork team had this answer:

We know from a lot of experiments that have been done in psychology since the 1950s that if someone looks at a hazy image, an ambiguous image, then they are going to interpret what they see, they are going to make up their own best guesses as to what they are looking at. We also know that if you stare at something for any length of time your eyes will become hazy. So if you stare at a statue for a couple of minutes without blinking your eyes too much, that statue is going to become rather hazy in outline to you and you will not be seeing the fine detail, and it is very possible that you might start to interpret what you see according to what you want to see.

On investigation it transpired that people had seen the statue move before but until the summer of 1985 no-one had made a big issue of these optical illusions. Why then had Madonna Mania broken out when it did?

The shrewd local postmaster Daniel Costello made this observation:

> People have shown an interest in the supernatural when times have been hard. In times of prosperity it's a case of God is in his heaven and all is right with the world, but then in times of recession, as now, when their whole way of life is upset, it is time to look to a more supernatural approach to their dilemma. I have heard that after the war in Italy, three hundred statues moved, and whether that was the Virgin in Heaven trying to console her people or what, I don't know.

The Roman Catholic Church always approaches supernatural sightings with some caution. It likes to keep control of the spiritual lives of the faithful and to guide them in the way it sees fit, and does not like to be sidetracked by what it would see as ephemeral manifestations of excessive folk piety. The local Roman Catholic bishop, Michael Murphy, Bishop of Cork and Ross, did not wish to give to the events at Ballinspittle the stamp of church approval by visiting the shrine. However, he confirmed that in Ireland that summer a new excitement had returned to church life, and he said that much good had followed from people meeting at the grottoes.

> They are very prayerful gatherings, very devotional, and I also know that the effect has been very good

for quite a number of people. Direct divine or supernatural intervention in the affairs of men is extremely rare and for that reason one has to approach any alleged appearances or movements with caution. It is common sense that one would first of all want to be sure that all possible natural explanations are exhausted before the Church would decide there had been some divine intervention. There have been similar instances in the past, and as you know it is reaching almost epidemic proportions at the moment, sightings of the kind. I think that by waiting things might clarify themselves. If we had to set up a commission for all the reported movements of statues and encounters with the Blessed Virgin we would be working overtime.

If the Bishop was not going to rush in and endorse the sightings as of God, he had to have some way of explaining why there was, to use his own expression, 'almost an epidemic' of moving statues.

First of all we have had a very bad summer, a very depressing summer. People haven't been able to go to the beach, haven't been able to go swimming. It must have been awful for people in caravans with children. And here is this thing suddenly reported in the media which people have seen. People's curiosity was naturally aroused and Ballinspittle was a place to go. The other thing of course is that we are living in a very difficult time in Ireland. We have very high unemployment, which is a very depressing

136

factor – especially for the individuals who are unemployed. It is very, very serious. Within the Church there is a certain questioning of accepted values, matters of faith; and then too there is the threat of nuclear destruction, felt by young people very much I think. They wonder if it is worthwhile putting in all the work to prepare for a profession. People generally may be in need of some sign of reassurance.

Bishop Murphy accepted that the sightings contained in them a message for the leaders of the Church. The people of Ireland, he said, were hungry for a spirituality of their own.

Since Vatican II there has been great emphasis on the intellectual side of things, discussion on various matters pertaining to the Church and belief. Some of this may well have passed over the heads of people. Not enough attention was paid to the emotional side of religion, and certainly there had been no attempt at promoting a genuine lay spirituality and a genuine popular devotion.

The popular devotion to the moving statues, like the popular devotion to so many of the extraordinary events of Christian history, did not last long. By the end of the summer of 1985 the crowds had begun to drift away from Ballinspittle. The novelty had worn off and everything came to an abrupt end when the statue, the object of devotion and wonder, was smashed by some Protestant fanatics.

The story of an Irish statue might not seem directly relevant to a study of stigmata, except that there is a well-attested story of a reported miracle, attached to this century's best known stigmatic, which can be directly attributed to an optical illusion. As in Ballinspittle the illusion was seen by a susceptible crowd willing a miracle to happen. It happened as Padre Pio was celebrating Mass, and an account of the event was given by Father Michael Hollings in a 1968 BBC television documentary about the famous stigmatic.

I'm a great believer in miracles, but I don't really think they're important. I think you want really to look back at Christ and see what he did. Normally he performed miracles for a particular purpose, to restore somebody's faith or to prove the point of who he was. Perhaps this could be the same attitude with regard to Padre Pio. I think he could have worked miracles, I've no doubt of that at all, but to me he didn't work any. The only time that I was really involved in the sort of thing which gets things distorted, was when I was serving the Mass. At a particular time, just before the communion, the Host is broken. Padre Pio's hands were sore. He broke the Host and the Host fell into the chalice.

I saw the Host in the chalice when I gave him water for the ablutions after the communion, and there it was. As soon as we arrived out of the church afterwards, my companion and I, everyone said: 'Miracolo, Miracolo!' So we said, 'Why?' 'The Host was there, and then it was gone!' So we said, 'No, it wasn't' – and so a miracle had occurred, which in fact had not occurred. There is always the danger of this sort of thing happening. But from what I heard when I was there myself, and from talking to some of the members of the community, and from talking to doctors, I would think that some of the miracles attributed to Padre Pio would be verifiable if and when they get to doing something about his canonization.

The stigmata is extraordinary in itself, yet in addition almost all cases have gathered to them or have had associated with them other extraordinary claims. Whether any of these claims can be described as miraculous depends very much on the understanding of that word. A miracle does not necessarily imply that the laws of nature have been broken. The word is popularly used in a sense that implies no supernatural involvement. 'Miracle escape of child from plane crash' would be a headline accompanying a newspaper story about an amazing and fortuitous event which in no way implied the child had been plucked by a supernatural force from the wreckage.

There are without doubt cases of inexplicable healing. People have remissions of illness which the medical profession cannot explain. The power of the mind over the body is immense and not fully understood. The term 'miracle' tends to be applied to events which do not involve supernatural forces, but the operations of laws of nature which at the time are not perhaps fully understood. Even a hundred years ago the modern world would have been unimaginable. That people could fly the Atlantic or have instantaneous communication by telephone and television would have attracted the description 'miraculous'.

There is no one simple explanation for the additional mystical phenomena associated with the stigmata. Each event would have to be examined closely in its own right. It is then probable that even reports of levitation or bilocation would eventually yield to an explanation which would satisfy the natural scientist. That explanation might involve an understanding of group psychology or even hypnotism. It would probably be inadequate to examine it solely in physical terms. Hypnotism, whether group or individual, might certainly provide a key. One explanation, for instance, of the Indian rope trick, which to witnesses appears to defy gravity, involves an understanding of a subtle use of hypnotism. One account tells of the trick being performed with the rope appearing to stand upright of its own accord and a boy climbing until he disappeared from view, and completely convincing the sceptical witness. That is, until he developed the film in the camera he had with him which showed no evidence of any rope being suspended in the air and no boy climbing it. The witness concluded he must have been hypnotized, without his knowledge, into believing that he saw what he expected to see.

It is a common game played by stage hypnotists to hand onions to the dozen or so volunteers susceptible to his suggestion and appearing on stage with him, and to tell them that the onions are in fact apples. The volunteers eat the onions with enjoyment, fully believing they are fruit. It is only at the end of the evening they realize what they have done and find the taste of onion in their mouths.

It might, however, be argued that this is an unsatis-factory explanation, as while hypnotism might work on small groups of suggestible subjects, it can hardly be expected to work with large crowds. However at a gathering of people awaiting a religious miracle, those present will not be just a cross-section of society, a random sample of believers and nonbelievers alike. They will be a self-selected sample of believers willing the miracle to take place and hoping to witness it.

Yet this viewpoint is still not entirely satisfactory. How does one explain the American journalists' seeing Father Bruse's weeping statues? It is possible that they fell victim to an elaborate conjuring trick. Indeed, Father Bruse and his congregation might all have been victims, and there have certainly been cases proven of miracles or supernatural events associated with inanimate objects which have been traced to hoaxes. One good example of this has been the phenomenon of the crop circles in Britain. For a number of years in the late '80s and early '90s curious patterns were found marked out in fields of corn, particularly in southern England. Many theories were put forward as to how they were caused. Some people were firmly convinced that a non-human intelligence was attempting to make contact. By the summer of 1993 it appeared fairly certain that all the patterns in the fields had been created by human beings. For several years there had been a number of small groups of hoaxers at work, independent of each other, but deriving a mischievous delight from their hobby. Two of the hoaxers owned up: Doug Bower and Dave Chorley claimed they had made dozens of circles, starting in 1975.

Some of the crop-circle enthusiasts refused to believe that these two mature gentlemen could have been responsible for fooling so many by wandering around in circles in fields, flattening the corn with an old plank. There might be a few hoaxers at work, they reasoned, but some of the corn circles were so incredible they had to have a more exotic origin. Yet this confidence in the existence of non-human agencies has been further undermined by the identification of others playing the same game. There are the Wessex Skeptics based at Southampton University, who have used a garden roller to make their imprints in farmers' fields. Then there is a person known as The Snake, based in Oxford, who started work in 1962 and is motivated into making circles, it is said, by fun, artistic pride and an irrational compulsion. He specializes in the complex pictograms which have been inadvertently praised by the enthusiasts as some of the most important crop formations.

Is it possible, however, to explain away all mysterious phenomena as hoaxes, hypnosis or the willing self-deception of observers? Are there not some phenomena which have no simple explanation and can only be attributed to the paranormal? It is possible that the well observed phenomenon of the poltergeist is truly paranormal. It has, however, very seldom been recorded on film or tape, and there is little evidence which can be dispassionately examined to show conclusively that objects have been thrown around rooms and floated in the air in defiance of gravity without the intervention of human beings. Nevertheless reliable witnesses have seen curious things happen and many of these events have been associated with individual people who appear to exert an influence on their surroundings quite inadvertently. Poltergeists in particular are associated with young girls at puberty. The theory has been floated, although nothing scientific has yet been measured, that people at certain stages in their life can radiate a form of invisible influence on the physical world around. If this was ever shown to be the case, the term 'paranormal' to describe the associated events would have to be replaced. Science would have to introduce a new term to imply that the events were accepted and understood and, although rare, were within the bounds of normality. In such an event it could well be that some of the miracles associated with mystical phenomena such as stigmata could be reinterpreted, and that it might be shown one day that the human being undergoing a profound religious experience can have an effect on the physical world around. It is now no longer a mystery to us that electromagnetic forces exist, and magnetism and radio waves can be very precisely harnessed. There is still much to learn about the universe.

There is even more to learn about ourselves, our minds and a possible collective consciousness. Is there in some way a shared memory? Are we as humans, at times of great stress or heightened emotion, able to reach beyond our normal capacities and capabilities? Is it perhaps only in exceptional times or in the presence of exceptional people that the miraculous can occur, or do we all have the capability within ourselves to reach beyond our normal boundaries of existence?

In the epilogue to his study of miracles C. S. Lewis put the view that God does not shake miracles into nature at random.

They come on great occasions: they are found at the great ganglions of history – not of political or social history, but of that spiritual history which cannot be fully known by men. If your own life does not happen to be near one of those great ganglions, how should you expect to see one? If we were heroic missionaries, apostles or martyrs, it would be a different matter. But why you or I? Unless you live near a railway, you will not see trains go past your windows. How likely is it that you or I will be present when a peace-treaty is signed, when a great scientific discovery is made, when a dictator commits suicide? That we should see a miracle is even less likely. Nor, if we understand, shall we be anxious to do so. 'Nothing almost sees miracles but misery.' Miracles and martyrdoms tend to bunch about the same areas of history – areas we have naturally no wish to frequent.

It is the case, however, that many instances of the stigmata have occurred in the hands and feet of very ordinary people, to whom they came quite unexpectedly. Cloretta Robinson sitting in her classroom at junior school was not at any great turning point of history, neither was Jane Hunt at home in Codnor. Would this have suggested to C. S. Lewis that their marks were not miraculous, or was something far more significant going on around them, something which will only become apparent at a distance of time, to which two ordinary people were inadvertently reacting?

The medical parallels can only give a partial understanding of the reality of stigmata. As has been seen, in only one case of psychogenic purpura did a patient produce on her own body replicated wounds that had originally occurred to someone else. However, in the case of stigmata all recipients produce wounds in empathy with the suffering of someone other than themselves, namely Christ. Also as far as psychogenic purpura is concerned, although a pattern of psychiatric symptoms emerged, there was no general report of patients having hallucinations or hearing voices.

In the case of stigmatics, the hearing of voices and the seeing of visions is a consistent and common accompaniment. Indeed, the more one examines both the contemporary cases and those of history, the form the visions take appears to be similar and consistent with each other. This could be used as evidence to suggest that the visions and the voices therefore come from one source, namely God. Yet that would be a view difficult to sustain. Important details differ from case to case. If a vision of Christ crucified was indeed a vision that came from God and was akin to newsreel footage of the events which occurred in Jerusalem around A.D. 33, it might be assumed that the visions would be consistent with each other and known historical facts. However, while most stigmatics have reported a vision of Christ's hand wounds bearing nail marks in the palms, more recently wounds in the wrists have been seen. This is clearly an inconsistency. One version must be historically inaccurate. Nail prints in the palms was the old image of crucifixion, and wrist injuries a more modern understanding of the nature of that form of execution. Indeed, it was only when it was realized that wrist wounds were more historically correct that these images began to appear. Very often the imagery that the person reproduces on his or her body corresponds to something with which he or she is already familiar, a religious picture or illustrated Bible.

Also it can be argued that frequently the voices heard have brought messages which have been surprisingly shallow and benign. They have consisted of general admonitions to the world and calls for repentance and closeness to Christ, but no stigmatic has ever yet come forward with messages as pertinent and powerful as the original messages of the Gospel. If the words of the stigmatics were truly those of God would not the messages be far more profound?

Frequently too stigmata is accompanied by vivid scenes of the Passion of Christ in front of the stigmatic's eyes. Or in other cases it is a vivid vision of Christ or the Virgin Mary. Sometimes stigmatics have drawn what they have seen. While some reports of these dreams might have become exaggerated in their telling, there is no reason to suggest that the first-hand accounts of visions have not been told in good faith.

Without doubt a normal mind is capable of creating images. Under hypnosis a subject can be persuaded to see almost anything. A trick once used by a stage hypnotist involved the subjects being persuaded that the hypnotist himself was invisible. When this happened and the hypnotist came on stage with a broom and began sweeping, the subjects reacted as if they were seeing a broom moving across the stage as if by itself, supported by no one. Some found this intriguing and began to examine the broom, others were alarmed by what they saw. It caused great hilarity to the audience.

It is certainly known that the mind and the eye together can play some curious tricks. Many optical illusions have been developed to confuse the eye, and there are numerous reports of people seeing things which they have incorrectly interpreted. Witnesses to crimes, when asked to recall what they have seen, often confuse two events and, without intentionally wanting to mislead, describe scenes which never existed.

In the curious state between sleep and awareness, confusions can arise, with, so it would seem, the world of the dream being superimposed upon the reality of the world. It is not difficult to understand how a vision might therefore occur. It is as if a person, although awake, is simultaneously dreaming and taking out of the imagination images which to themselves appear very real. It might also be the case that the human mind is capable of some form of sympathetic reasoning, or thought transference, and that telepathy, although not understood, can in some circumstances exist. Accepting this, it would not be difficult to understand how two people perhaps might have a similar vision together. At Medjugorge when the children go forward and see the Virgin Mary, although the crowds do not see the same vision yet they do not disbelieve the children. It is generally accepted that some people will see a vision and others next to them in the room will not. The stigmatics, however, have tended to see their visions alone. Jane Hunt, who saw the Virgin Mary in her house, says that her husband, in the same room, saw nothing.

When it comes to some of the more extraordinary stories such as bilocation, again one can take a rational approach. A person thinking of Padre Pio, or having some unconscious memory of the friar, might well conjure up an image of Pio at a time of need. Seeing this vision could be interpreted as a case of bilocation: Padre Pio would be at St Giovanni Rotondo even though the vision, conjured up by the third party, would be somewhere else. Also if a third party came to see Padre Pio, being in some form of distress, they might well find that their problems were resolved in their own mind, just by being in the presence of the friar. In other words, people making their confessions to Padre Pio would have sorted out their problems in their own minds by focusing on them as they waited to see him. And at the moment they met him, a moment they had been eagerly awaiting with the highest expectations, all would come clear. And because of the priest's reputation they would attribute that clarity to an extraordinary insight of the priest.

This is not to belittle the role of Padre Pio, or claim in any way that what he was doing was not valid, it is to root legend in reality. Once a reputation is inflated, justifiably or otherwise, there is a tendency for unusual events to be interpreted in extraordinary ways and for the more basic and simple explanations to be overlooked. Again, according to one's understanding of such matters, it would still be quite possible to say that this was the way God works on earth. He does not overrule his creative laws, but uses them to the full. Again some will argue that all events, even the mundane and trivial, and certainly the uplifting and miraculous, were pre-ordained, or programmed into the world at the point of creation. And this was done by the creator – God.

It is frequently the case that the legend has more power than the reality. Indeed the real truth lies in the legend and not in the historical event. If, as might have been the case with Padre Pio and reports of his unusual body temperature, a faulty thermometer was used by a medic to take his temperature and that thermometer broke, the obvious explanation that the thermometer was at fault would have been overlooked, and reports would have developed about the mystic's amazing body heat. This would have fitted in with the whole pattern of the man being something out of the ordinary. This would have developed into a legend which would have fitted in with other legends of great mystics being able to sustain high body temperatures. It could be argued that because these stories of high body temperatures are not uncommonly associated with great mystics this must have something to do with their mysticism. On the other hand, many thousands of people have at some time had unusually raised body temperatures. Normally this is put down to a medical cause and there is no question of a mystical interpretation being involved. It is only when the person in question has attracted to them other curious tales that the raised temperature is seen to be significant.

Some amazing reports concern St Catherine of Genoa who lived between 1447 and 1510. It was said of her that in addition to her body after death remaining undecomposed and one of her arms elongating in a peculiar manner shortly before her death, the blood from her stigmata gave off exceptional heat.

Baron Friedrich von Hügel, her biographer, wrote of one incident in her life.

There was a day when she suffered such an intensity of burning that it was impossible to keep her in bed. She seemed like a creature placed in a great flame of fire, so much so that human eyes could not endure the spectacle of such martyrdom. This anguish lasted a whole day and night and it was impossible to touch her skin because of the acute pain which she felt from any such touch.

In her day there was no objective way of measuring the heat, and her experience of temperature was of necessity subjective. It could have been her own accounts of feeling herself to be burning which led to the later legends told about her and her heated blood.

To search for and find explanations for the stigmata and associated events, which might satisfy the sceptics, is not to dismiss mystical phenomena as illusion or superstition. The stories of these happenings and the power of these stories to sustain and strengthen faith is what is important. In the same way that modern folk tales of, for instance, bogus social workers calling on the unsuspecting to inspect their children, might express dormant anxieties about authority and produce fear in a community, so tales of extraordinary religious events can release dormant spirituality and produce a Christian revival. To say that religious folk myths are products of human society is not to say that the tradition of faith from which they are drawn is not valid. In the way that the stigmata are an individual's psychosomatic response to a religious experience, so the reports of the associated mystical phenomena are the community's response to a similar religious experience. It is not a case of God overriding the laws of nature. That would involve a curious understanding of God and rule out the possibility of God being a loving God. Why should he play mystical party games with his human creatures and ignore the suffering world? Surely, using his supposed supernatural abilities, he could alleviate drought and famine through his direct intervention.

The Rev. David Lockyer, as well as being the spiritual mentor to Ethel Chapman, was also in charge of a parish near to where she lived. It was based around a housing estate which had all the problems of unemployment and poverty of the time. Unemployment stood at 35 per cent, and only twelve members of his two worshipping communities were wage-earning people. He asked himself the question, why did God appear to ignore the suffering in his parish and yet decide to intervene in the world by implanting the stigmata on a disabled recluse? The answer to the question lay in understanding that God did not ignore the suffering and had not intervened in his world to produce a sort of mystical conjuring trick. As a result of knowing Ethel, David Lockyer wrote this:

> Being involved with Ethel and the stigmata, I have come across a basically simple soul who has suffered, who has been the victim of circumstances beyond her control and yet has been able to find a meaning and purpose to life and a depth of communion with the ground of her being.

151

It hasn't answered all the problems, but it has redressed the balance. It has been a sign to me which has rooted me back to the centrality of the cross. Even if things are stacked against one, I had in Ethel an example of someone who was prepared to surrender her life entirely to the hands of God.

I've gone to Ethel sometimes when I felt absolutely low and said, 'How are you today?' and I know full well she has been suffering either with her multiple sclerosis or her diabetes or her inner thoughts, and there's been that smile on her face, and she's said, 'Oh, you're suffering too, are you? I can see by your face, let's have a talk together.'

And I've gone away, and she's done more for me than I've done for her.

And there is an argument that even if all of Ethel's experiences, her stigmata, healing, premonition, odour of sanctity and so on, can be explained in terms of the laws of nature, that is not to dismiss their divine origin, as all natural laws are laws of God. The answer to the question, 'Did Ethel's stigmata come from God?', or to widen it out and ask 'Have any non-fraudulent stigmata come from God?' is one that no one can answer for someone else. The followers of St Francis, the family of Maria de Moerl, the physicians who examined Dorothy Kerin, the crowds who gathered at Padre Pio's Masses will all have answered the question in their own ways.

How those questions are answered depends entirely on the individual's perception of God. Is God the collective name given to the forces of nature, everything in this world and beyond, even those beyond the comprehension of people? Is he the awesome omnipotent power to be feared and obeyed? Is he the creator who put in place at the beginning the miracles to come? Or is he the loving father and personal saviour who can guide, direct and intervene in the lives of each and every one of us? Each one of us must decide for ourselves which image is the one that best expresses our own personal relationship with and understanding of the same God. And on the answers each one of us finds, will rest our own explanation for and comprehension of the stigmata.

Epilogue

It would never be possible to complete a study of a living subject like the stigmata and state categorically that the mystery had been solved. Each experience of the stigmata is unique and new cases regularly emerge to replace those that pass into history. Each new case discovered raises new questions about the condition which need to be answered.

Since completing the preceding chapters in the summer of 1993, a number of events have occurred which have broadened the understanding of the condition and have suggested new solutions to the mysteries posed.

In the Republic of Ireland the mystic and prophetess Christina Gallagher has been confirmed as a stigmatist. At Achill Sound, a remote part of western Ireland, Christina is at the centre of a religious revival. Responding to a vision of the Virgin Mary, the County Mayo housewife set up a house of prayer at Achill to which hundreds of visitors now make pilgrimage. They come to meet Christina, to seek her counsel, and to take part in a religious movement which believes that the world should turn from its sinful ways in preparation for a "chastisement" which will take place by the year 2000.

Christina reports many visions of heaven and hell. She sees apparitions of Christ and Our Lady. The Our Lady Queen of Peace House of Prayer is a renovated convent, highly decorated with religious images and symbols. At a small shop, through which all the visitors pass, it is possible to buy rosaries, statuettes, and copies of a special medal which Christina has had struck according to a design she saw in one of her visions.

At the end of 1993 Christina agreed to talk for the first time on television about her experience, which now includes that of stigmata. Now in her forties, Christina was brought up a Roman Catholic and there was little that was exceptional about her, although unusually when she left school and took her first job in domestic service, she was unable to read and write. She recalls a time when she prayed, amongst other things, for the ability to read and how quite suddenly she discovered that she could understand a newspaper and began to write her name and compose sentences.

Her visions, which began in 1985, are vivid. Later, over time, she developed the pain of the stigmata. In the television interview she said that she felt pain ninety percent of the time and described one occasion when the pain in her head was so acute she felt that she was about to die. "It was as if thorns were being pierced through my head. I saw flashes of the face of Jesus and called out to him for the pain to stop."

She has also received, briefly, marks on her wrists corresponding to the marks of crucifixion, and in early 1994 film was taken of bleeding wounds on her forehead corresponding to a crown of thorns. Others at the House of Prayer have frequently spoken of seeing Christina in a state of ecstatic prayer or intense suffering.

Christina talks of being aware of the presence of Padro Pio and her guardian angel, and slowly there is a cult growing up around her. Priests who visit talk of her amazing insight into their souls and problems. She has produced thousands of words of prophecy and the Roman Catholic Church is taking her experience very seriously. A priest is assigned to her as a spiritual adviser and, although in its usual way it is remaining officially cautious. Christina has had visits from Church leaders and has had meetings with, amongst others, Mother Teresa of Calcutta.

For Christina the stigmata are but one outward sign of a much wider spiritual experience. As the end of the century—indeed, the millenium approaches—she is one of a number of people around the world who have become focal points of apocalyptic prophecy. On display at the shop at the House of Prayer in Achill is information about at least two other people like Christina, including Sister Agnes Sasagawa in Japan and Julia Kim in Korea. In the case of Sister Agnes, in 1973 she developed a pain in her hand which developed into a wound in the shape of a cross. In a vision she was told by the Virgin Mary that she would be healed of her deafness and was asked by Mary to make reparation for the sins of mankind. Over the following years other extraordinary events occurred around Sister Agnes and hundreds of witnesses claim they saw a statue of the Virgin Mary weep.

Similar events occurred thirteen years later in Korea

associated with Julia Kim. There a statue of Mary wept blood. Julia Kim believed that her special calling, given to her by the Virgin Mary in a vision, was to suffer on behalf of the souls of children who had been aborted as embryos. In July 1988 her body began to swell and she experienced, in a state of religious ecstasy, the pain of giving birth. This phantom pregnancy and labour was, her followers claimed, to draw attention to the Catholic view on abortion.

In addition to new cases of stigmata , important experimental work has been undertaken within the last two years by an Italian doctor and psychotherapist, Marco Margnelli. He was instrumental in uncovering Michele Improta as a fraud, but also he was involved in confirming the "genuine" psychosomatic nature of the curious stigmata of Domenica Lo Bianco, a stigmatist from the south of Italy. When Michele Improta came to him at the height of Improta's fame, he was introduced to Dr. Margnelli as Virginia Improta. For as well as claiming the stigmata, Improta was also claiming to be a woman. The first test that Dr. Margnelli carried out was to determine Improta's gender, and an X-ray examination revealed that Improta had false breasts. A hormone examination showed the high level of testosterone associated with a man.

Margnelli saw dramatic videotapes and photographs of Improta's stigmatisation, including marks on the hands and on the face and vivid writing in blood on his pillow with the word "Maria" being prominent.

Once Dr. Margnelli had uncovered Improta's dubious gender, his subject became far less willing to be examined. He failed to return for further tests on the stigmata and the observations that Margnelli was able to make revealed no apparent marks. For a while Improta was at the centre of a cult, with hundreds of devotees crowding into his village to hear him speak. However, his public became disillusioned following one episode in which he prophesied the day of his death and then asked his followers to pray that he might be spared. When, in fact, he did not die, Improta lost public credibility. He later disappeared from general view.

"We did, however, perform a careful study of his psychology," said Dr. Margnelli, "and had the opportunity to carry out some hypnotic sessions during which we tried to reproduce his mystical phenomena with hypnosis. We had no success—no ecstasy, no stigmata, nothing at all. Careful photographic tests showed no evidence of wounds or scarring, and we asked many times that he come back to us and show us the phenomena when they appeared. But we had no answer from him. He is said to perform miracles. A lot of people go to look at him and he prays like a priest. But in my view he is a liar."

Marco Margnelli, however, is not a general sceptic. He has been involved in experiments which have verified the nonfraudulent psychosomatic nature of one stigmatic. Domenica Lo Bianco receives religious symbols on her left arm every Good Friday. They consist of a cross and rosary and what might be construed as stars. Videotape was taken in 1992 of Domenica lying in bed in a state of religious ecstasy on Good Friday with the marks appearing on her arms. When Marco Margnelli examined her, however, it was many months after that experience and the stigmata had vanished. He interviewed her at length with four others and the whole episode was recorded on camera and photographed. At one point during the psycho-examination, Domenica became distressed and went into a trance-like state. It was then, Dr. Mangnelli, his colleagues, and video tape confirm, that the marks that had vanished many months earlier on her arm began to reappear. Over the course of an hour they became distinctive red marks of a cross and a rosary, even though at that time she was not at any point left by herself, and witnesses confirmed that the marks reappeared without any external assistance.

"It was a most important happening," Dr. Margnelli said. "During our tests and examination she started with a normal skin and at the end of our enquiry the stigmata had become visible. From the time when her skin was clear through to the time when the marks emerged, she was under our constant observation. It took about one hour."

The experiment is similar to one conducted in the nineteenth century on Louise Lateau in which her arm was encased by doctors in a solid-glass cylinder over a period of twenty-four hours. During that time her wounds were expected to become active and indeed they did. The doctors satisfied themselves that the hemorrhages occurred spontaneously and without the intervention of external violence.

What Dr. Margnelli and Louise Lateau's medical observers were able to demonstrate conclusively was that wounds can emerge psychosomatically. What these experiments could not determine was whether wounds can only re-emerge psychosomatically. Do the original wounds have to be made physically even though subsequently they can be repeated without physical aid?

In an early-twentieth-century case the psychologist

Dr. Pierre Janet described the case of a woman called Madeleine. He conducted an experiment in which he bandaged her foot in such a way that her wounds could be seen through a piece of glass. He noticed some redness and a lesion emerging, but would not conclude that this was a spontaneous stigma, as he could not rule out the possibility that it did not represent some pre-existing traumatic injury.

It is impossible to be sure that on the very first occasion stigmata occur on any individual that it is entirely a spontaneous event, as no one has ever been present when marks have first emerged. The nearest to that position was when Ethel Chapman was in hospital and her wounds appeared under medical supervision. There is, however, no way of being able to determine that the medical supervision was constant. In theory the wounds could have been produced in some physical manner, not deliberately, but unconsciously, when the medical staff were not present.

Both Dr. Margnelli's current work and his historical research have shown that what all stigmatists have had in common is an experience of an altered state of consciousness. It was significant that Domenica's wounds re-emerged when she was in a trance-like state. Whether in the visions or trances which they have described, all the stigmatics share this characteristic. Christina Gallagher experiences periods of religious ecstasy, as did Heather Woods, George Hamilton, Jane Hunt, and all of those recent cases which have been examined in detail. Thus, if the psychosomatic element of the emergence of stigmata is associated with altered states of consciousness, by exploring these altered states one can arrive at some understanding of the mechanism by which stigmata occur.

A stage hypnotist can, for the entertainment of an audience, produce amusing and bizarre behaviour in the volunteers who take part in his act. First the hypnotist must
select the volunteers carefully and rule out those who are
not suggestible. With a well-chosen half-dozen or so, he
can proceed with an act which often borders on the
bizarre. Subjects can appear to believe that they are in
other places and seeing things which do not exist. They
can be told to eat onions and believe that they are peaches.
They can be told to believe that the hypnotist is invisible
and are alarmed when they see an object that he is carrying
chasing them, apparently of its own volition, around the
stage. It is also claimed by stage hypnotists that if they
touch a person with an inert object on the body, it can
have an effect on their skin. This effect has more to do
with what that person believes they have been touched
with, rather than the object itself. The British stage hypnotist Ashley Dean says that if he touches a person who is
allergic to wool on the arm with any material other than
wool, but tells him that in fact it is wool, he will get an
allergy rash. Also he says that he has seen someone have a
coin placed on his hand and be told that the coin is red
hot. The pain of burning has been felt and a red weal
emerges when the coin is moved.

Perhaps this suggests there are both psychosomatic and
physical origins of the stigmata. If in a state of ecstasy, a
form perhaps of auto-hypnosis, that person believes that
he is himself crucified or suffering alongside with Christ,
he may place a finger or an object on his hands or his feet
unknowingly, convince himself that what he is feeling is a

nail being driven in, and receive a corresponding wound.

Once the initial marks have been made, they may or may not be consciously maintained by the stigmatist. Since, in a number of cases, marks have disappeared completely, it would suggest that perhaps once the person has decided no longer to maintain the marks himself, the marks naturally disappear and heal. As Padro Pio grew weaker in his old age, his marks gradually disappeared. Some would say this was in accordance with a miraculous plan; others might project that as the priest became weaker, it was harder for him to physically maintain the standard of his marks. Certainly in his youth he had used iodine on the wounds which had served both to disinfect and exacerbate the evidence.

In the words of one doctor who examined Padre Pio, his marks "are also due to the use of known chemical agents (tincture of old iodine, which because of the iodidric acid that develops in it, become very caustic and irritating). It would be a 'multiple neurotic necrosis of the skin perhaps unconsciously caused by a phenomenon of suggestion.' artifically maintained by the use of chemicals." The supporters of Padre Pio will point out that the priest did not use iodine all his life and yet the marks persisted.

Stigmata are now a world-wide phenomenon. Once they had been a localised experience of a few pious people living in the Mediterranean region and belonging to the Roman Catholic Church. Now the idea and the inspiration for the marks has spread around the world and to other denominations as well.

In that the stigmata must always be seen in a social context, it is possible that as the end of the millenium approaches and, like Christina Gallagher, more and more people believe that an end time is near, more people will want to suffer for Christ to help redeem the sins of what they see as a fallen and wicked world. Christina Gallagher describes herself as a "victim soul." Once in a vision she saw Christ, who asked her for a drink of water. "But how am I to give you this water?" she asked. Jesus replied, "You are like a grape, ripe. When you are crushed, that juice refreshes me; I am thirsty for souls."

Christina Gallagher sees it as her role to suffer through her stigmata for the sins of the world, as one of those chosen especially today to experience something of Christ's suffering. Heather Woods too felt that she had an urgent message for her time. Other modern stigmatists have felt they have had a more localised call to heal the sick or stir up a church revival.

Others continue to experience the wounds as a personal act of devotion or private sorrow. George H. in Glasgow, who early in 1994 spoke on television about his experience for the first time and is now known publicly to be George Hamilton from the Ruchazie district, described his stigmata as "more of a curse than a blessing." His physician, Dr. John Spence, also appeared with George, confirming that his patient was not the sort of person who in his view would have deliberately marked himself. However, George reacted curiously to the publicity he received. On one hand he was willing to tell his story and give his friends and neighbours the opportunity to understand what it was he was going through. On the other hand at the height of the interest from local newspapers a photograph of him was taken with his face streaked in blood and other marks showing on his body which did not relate to his stigmata. Medically they showed all the signs of self-mutilation, but George insisted he had no knowledge of how the marks appeared and told how he woke up one morning to find himself in the condition. The Roman Catholic Church, too, has taken his case more seriously, and Bishop John Mone of Paisley has said that while he does not endorse any claim that George's marks have come from God, he, on behalf of the Church, is most willing to listen carefully to George and believe what he says he has been through.

The life of a stigmatic will always be difficult. Even the celebrated Padre Pio wrote of times of great despair. After an intense outburst of stigmatic activity and visions in 1993, Heather Woods became acutely depressed, and for a while felt that she had been abandoned by God. In November 1993 she died. Her body had been found in a river near her home. An inquest into her death returned an open verdict that there was not sufficient evidence to prove that she had been either a victim of an accident or had taken her own life. At an autopsy her hands and feet were examined and no evidence was found that in the areas where her stigmata had been active had any implement been used to make the wounds or any artificial dyes injected. These were two possible explanations for her wounds which the investigating coroner wished to test.

In all probability throughout the world over the coming years there will be an increase in stigmatists. Indeed the last ten years of this century could see a peak of activity. Up until now this particular mystical phenomenon has been reported on average by a dozen people at any one time. This decade that figure of twelve or so will in all probability multiply considerably. In the course of compiling this book, I have seen the numbers risen to around twenty.

The more cases that come forward for examination, the more the mechanism by which the marks appear will become clear to doctors. But whether the marks are entirely psychosomatic, partly physical, or entirely physical, or even in some cases bordering on the fraudulent, the mechanism by which the marks appear would seem to be less important than the response made by people to the marks when they see them. For, providing there are people who believe that fraud does not exist in every case—and very few people believe that—the stigmata will always be viewed with wonder and awe, and trigger off in the minds of those who witness it a whole range of theological questions involving the nature of God and the relationship between God and all humankind.